GRÜNES LICHT

TRAINING FÜRS GYMNASIUM

Englisch 5. Klasse

Bayern

Cornelsen

Herausgeber: Bibliographisches Institut GmbH, Mannheim
Marketing & Vertrieb: Cornelsen Schulverlage Marketing GmbH, Berlin

Projektleitung und Reihenkonzeption: Annegret Hauser
Redaktion: Anja Sieber, Avinus Verlag & Lektoratsservice, Berlin
Illustration: Dorina Teßmann, Berlin
Umschlaggestaltung: tritopp, Berlin
Layoutkonzept: Dagmar und Torsten Lemme, Berlin
Layout und technische Umsetzung: Carola Fuchs, Berlin

www.cornelsen.de

1. Auflage 2012

Druck: Beltz Bad Langensalza GmbH

ISBN: 978-3-06-150195-2

Inhalt gedruckt auf säurefreiem Papier aus nachhaltiger Forstwirtschaft.

Hier finden Sie die systematische Übersicht der in diesem Band behandelten Themen.
Der Lernplan auf S. 9–11 kann für den eigenen Bedarf genutzt werden.

Die Autorinnen

Kristina Davis

Annette Haseneder

Sylvia Hochstrasser

Simone Huber

Beate Ruckdäschel

Andrea Schwarz

Ursula Schwoerer

Ute Walter

Einführung

Der vorliegende Band **Grünes Licht: Training fürs Gymnasium** unterstützt das Lernen im Englischunterricht der Jahrgangsstufe 5 am Gymnasium. Die Arbeit damit beugt Wissenslücken vor und gibt Gymnasialschülerinnen und -schülern Sicherheit im Unterricht sowie bei Tests und Schulaufgaben.

Aufbau: Arbeiten mit den Modulen

Der Englisch-Lernstoff des 5. Schuljahrs ist in **39 Trainings-** und **sechs Testmodulen** aufbereitet. Sie folgen unter sprachsystematischem Schwerpunkt der Unit-Progression der in Bayern wichtigen Englisch-Lehrwerke. Daher erfolgt die Unterteilung in die Teile A bis F, welche jeweils mit einem Test abgeschlossen werden.

12 | 1 Personal pronouns

Seite | Nummer des Moduls | Thema / Lernschwerpunkt des Moduls

Jedes Modul ist eine in sich geschlossene Einheit, die in etwa 30–45 Minuten bearbeitet werden kann. Alle Module bestehen aus:

- einer **Wissensseite** (zum Wiederholen und Festigen des im Unterricht Behandelten: mit Fakten, Regeln und Hinweisen),
- zwei **Aufgabenseiten** (mit *Exercises* zum Anwenden, Üben und Trainieren),
- einer **Lösungsseite** (der *Answer Key* enthält neben ausführlichen Lösungen bei Bedarf auch Hilfestellungen und weiterführende Kommentare).

36 | TEST A

Die Tests behandeln Inhalte der jeweils vorangehenden Modulgruppen, z. B. TEST A zu Teil A, bestehend aus den Modulen 1–6. Alle Tests enthalten ein Punktbewertungssystem und bestehen aus:

- vier **Aufgabenseiten,**
- einer **Lösungsseite.**

Einsatzmöglichkeiten

Das Trainingsmaterial eignet sich durch seinen klaren Aufbau zum selbstständigen Bearbeiten durch die Lernenden. Dieses kann nach dem jeweiligen Bedarf erfolgen:

- im kontinuierlich unterrichtsbegleitenden Lernen zu Hause,
- im Intensivierungsunterricht,
- bei spezifischem Förderbedarf nach Vorgaben und in Absprache mit der Lehrperson,
- zum individuellen Nachschlagen und Üben, Füllen von Wissenslücken sowie
- zur langfristigen Vorbereitung auf den Jahrgangsstufentest zu Beginn des 6. Schuljahrs.

Organisationshilfen

Die Arbeit mit diesem Trainingsmaterial kann, je nach individuellem Bedarf, über unterschiedliche Zugänge erfolgen:

- Das **Inhaltsverzeichnis** (S. 3–5) bietet dem unter sprachsystematisch-grammatischem Schwerpunkt Suchenden den schnellen Zugang zu allen entsprechenden Modulen und Seitenzahlen.
- Der **Lernplan** (S. 9–11) hilft bei der Planung und Organisation des Lernens. Hier kann die Englischlehrerin oder der Englischlehrer je nach Trainingsbedarf vermerken, welche Module und Tests bis wann bearbeitet werden sollen. Die Lernenden können die eigene Arbeit im Anschluss durch Auswahl und Zuordnung eines der drei Gesichter selbst beurteilen und dies bei Bedarf mit ihrer Lehrerin oder ihrem Lehrer besprechen. So ist der Lernplan aufgebaut:

Modul	Thema/Lernschwerpunkt	Seite	bitte bearbeiten zum:	☺ 😐 ☹

- Wer im Unterricht z. B. einen *Grammatical term* nicht richtig verstanden hat, findet im **Glossar** (S. 204–206) dessen deutsche Übersetzung, ein englisches Sprachbeispiel und außerdem die Nummern aller Module, die Faktenwissen und Aufgaben dazu enthalten.
- Ein durchgängiges Hilfsmittel ist die bei Wissens- und Aufgabenseiten die auf der rechten Seite mitlaufende **Randspalte**, in der Lernende ggf. unklare Punkte oder Rückfragebedarf markieren, die mit der Englischlehrerin oder dem Englischlehrer aufgegriffen werden können. Kann man überwiegend Häkchen in dieser Spalte setzen, wird der eigene Lernerfolg bewusst. ✓ ↩ ?

Tests

Die Tests können entweder abschließend nach vollständiger Bearbeitung der jeweils vorangehenden Modulgruppe durchlaufen werden (also z. B. TEST A nach Teil A, bestehend aus den Modulen 1–6). Alternativ sind sie zu Beginn, also zur einsteigenden Ermittlung des Leistungsstands bzw. des Übungsbedarfs nutzbar. Bereiche, in denen die erreichte Punktzahl nicht zufriedenstellend ist, können dann bevorzugt bearbeitet werden.
Das verwendete Punktbewertungssystem bildet die Benotung im Englischunterricht nicht 1:1 ab, sondern soll Lernenden eine realistische Groborientierung über den jeweiligen eigenen Stand ermöglichen. Der untere Wert des 😐 sichert etwa noch ein *Ausreichend;* die oberen Werte des ☺ entsprechen *guten* bzw. *sehr guten* Leistungen.

Audio-Downloads

🔊 Alle Tests sowie einige Trainingsmodule enthalten von englischen Muttersprachlerinnen und Muttersprachlern eingesprochene Dialoge und Hörtexte. Das nebenstehende Symbol verweist im Lernplan und bei der betreffenden *Exercise* auf kostenlose Audio-Downloads unter www.cornelsen.de/grueneslicht-englisch-bayern.
Hier sind neben den Audio-Dateien im MP3-Format auch die verschriftlichten Texte (Transkripte) im PDF-Format abruf- und ausdruckbar.

Viel Erfolg!

Module mit enthalten Audio-Downloads unter www.cornelsen.de/grueneslicht-englisch-bayern.

Module mit 🔊 enthalten Audio-Downloads unter www.cornelsen.de/grueneslicht-englisch-bayern.

Module mit enthalten Audio-Downloads unter www.cornelsen.de/grueneslicht-englisch-bayern.

1 Personal pronouns (Personalpronomen)

Ein ***personal pronoun*** *(Personalpronomen)* steht für ein Nomen, das als Subjekt des Satzes dient. Dieses Nomen kann eine Person oder ein Gegenstand sein. Im Deutschen spricht man auch von einem persönlichen Fürwort. Man verwendet es häufig, um den Namen einer Person nicht zu wiederholen: *John is my friend.* ***He*** *is very nice.*
Im Englischen gibt es folgende ***personal pronouns.***

singular		plural	
I	ich	***we***	wir
you	du	***you***	ihr/Sie
he	er		
she	sie	***they***	sie
it	es		

1 Personal pronouns: singular

Das ***personal pronoun*** in der 1. Person Singular ***I*** *(ich)* wird immer großgeschrieben. ***You*** heißt auf Deutsch sowohl *du* (Singular) als auch *ihr* (Plural). Auch in der Höflichkeitsform *(Sie)* wird es verwendet (Singular und Plural).

Are ***you*** *the new pupil?*	Bist **du** der neue Schüler?
You *are my best friends.*	**Ihr** seid meine besten Freunde.
Mr Morgan, can ***you*** *do that for me?*	Mr Morgan, können **Sie** das für mich tun?
Mr Smith and Mr Brown, can ***you*** *show me that?*	Mr Smith und Mr Brown, können **Sie** mir das zeigen?

Für eine weibliche Person steht ***she,*** für eine männliche Person steht ***he.***
She heißt also auf Deutsch *sie* (3. Person Singular).
☛ Das deutsche *sie* (3. Person Plural) heißt auf Englisch ***they.***

This is Jennifer. ***She*** *lives in my street.*	***3rd person singular***
Look at Christopher and Marc! What are ***they*** *doing?*	***3rd person plural***

Für ein Tier oder für eine Sache verwendet man im Unterschied zum Deutschen immer ***it.*** Für Tiere, die man gut kennt und deren Namen man weiß, verwendet man je nach Geschlecht ***he*** oder ***she.***

Woof, our dog, is very nice. ***He*** *often plays with me.*	*This is my cat, Aurora.* ***She*** *is so beautiful.*
Where is the dog? Is ***it*** *in the garden?*	*Our car is not very new;* ***it*** *is 12 years old.*

2 Personal pronouns: plural

Die englischen Pronomen im Plural heißen ***we, you*** und ***they.***

My family and I, ***we*** *live in a little town.*	*Jenny and Viola, where are* ***you?***
Emily's parents are very nice. On Sundays, ***they*** *go swimming together.*	

EXERCISE 1 Write a pronoun for the following names or nouns.

Mary and Anne	*they*	Peter	
my cat Cindy		my mother and I	
Jennifer		my uncle Robert	
my two brothers		our house	
our family		my best friends	

EXERCISE 2 Rewrite the sentences and use the correct **personal pronoun.**

1 Jessica isn't at school today.

____.

2 Peter and John are playing football in the garden.

____.

3 Tim's father works in his office.

____.

4 This dog is very lazy.

____.

5 Simon and I are going to Paris together.

____.

6 My teacher Mr Brown knows a lot of things.

____.

7 My brother's cat Annabel is 2 years old.

____..

EXERCISE 3 How do you translate **you** in these sentences?

	du	ihr	Sie
Mary, can you come and help me, please?			
Why are you not at work today, Mr Miller?			
Children, what are you doing?			
You cannot do this, Woof!			
How old are you, Harry?			
You are so nice, Mrs Smith.			
Can you come to my birthday party, Helen and Sue?			
You must do your homework, Jenny!			

Exercise 4 Complete the text. Use the correct translation of the following pronouns:

er er ich ich sie sie sie sie sie wir wir

Sarah tells us about a very special day: "Today I am very happy! It is my birthday and my family and I, ______ are going to the zoo! My uncle Henry is also coming. ______ is nice and ______ like uncle Henry, because ______ often plays with me. ______ have a lot of fun together! Christina, my best friend from school, is already there. ______ likes animals and ______ has two dogs: Woof and Poof! ______ are not very big and ______ are very sweet! ______ also like dogs, but my parents don't. ______ say that dogs are a lot of work."

Exercise 5 Be careful: **she** or **they?**

My sister is 13 years old. *She* likes pop music and chocolate. Where are Jimmy and his friends? Why aren't ________ at school today? The Millers are our neighbours and ________ live in a very big house. Mrs Smith is our English teacher and ________ is very funny: ________ always wears red shoes! I think ________ are very beautiful. The new pupil in our class, Helen, is from London. ________ has long hair and brown eyes.

Exercise 6 Translate the following sentences.

1 Sie haben viele Freunde.

____.

2 Du kannst mit Jessica spielen.

____.

3 Ist er dein Nachbar?

____.

4 Wie alt seid ihr?

____.

5 Sind Sie neu in London, Mr Teller?

____.

Exercise 1

Mary and Anne	**they**	Peter	**he**
my cat Cindy	**she**	my mother and I	**we**
Jennifer	**she**	my uncle Robert	**he**
my two brothers	**they**	our house	**it**
our family	**we**	my best friends	**they**

Exercise 2

1 **She** isn't at school today.
2 **They** are playing football in the garden.
3 **He** works in his office.
4 **It** is very lazy.
5 **We** are going to Paris together.
6 **He** knows a lot of things.
7 **She** is 2 years old.

Exercise 3

	du	ihr	Sie
Mary, can you come and help me, please?	✗		
Why are you not at work today, Mr Miller?			✗
Children, what are you doing?		✗	
You cannot do this, Woof!	✗		
How old are you, Harry?	✗		
You are so nice, Mrs Smith.			✗
Can you come to my birthday party, Helen and Sue?		✗	
You must do your homework, Jenny!	✗		

Exercise 4

Sarah tells us about a very special day:

"Today **I** am very happy! It is my birthday and my family and I, **we** are going to the zoo! My uncle Henry is also coming. **He** is nice and I like uncle Henry, because **he** often plays with me. **We** have a lot of fun together! Christina, my best friends from school, is already there. **She** likes animals and **she** has two dogs: Woof and Poof! **They** are not very big and **they** are very sweet! **I** also like dogs, but my parents don't. **They** say that dogs are a lot of work.

Exercise 5

My sister is 13 years old. **She** likes pop music and chocolate.
Where are Jimmy and his friend? Why aren't **they** at school today?
The Millers are our neighbours and **they** live in a very big house.
Mrs Smith is our English teacher and **she** is very funny: **she** always wears red shoes! I think **they** are very beautiful. The new pupil in our class, Helen, is from London. **She** has long hair and brown eyes.

Exercise 6

1 Sie haben viele Freunde.
They/You have a lot of friends.

2 Du kannst mit Jessica spielen.
You can play with Jessica.

3 Ist er dein Nachbar?
Is he your neighbour?

4 Wie alt seid ihr?
How old are you?

5 Sind Sie neu in London, Mr Teller?
Are you new in London, Mr Teller?

2 Possessive determiners (Possessivbegleiter)

Wörter wie ***my, your, his, her, its, our, your, their*** *(mein, dein, sein, ihr, unser, euer)* nennt man ***possessive determiners*** *(Possessivbegleiter* oder *besitzanzeigende Begleiter).* Sie geben an, zu wem etwas oder jemand gehört. Diese Possessivbegleiter beziehen sich auf die jeweiligen Personalpronomen in der entsprechenden Person: ***I – my, you – your*** usw.

personal pronouns	possessive determiners
I*'m not Ellen.*	***My*** *name is Helen.*
You*'re new.*	***Your*** *school bag is nice.*
He*'s from London.*	***His*** *house is over there.*
She*'s a teacher.*	***Her*** *subject is German.*
It*'s a budgie.*	***Its*** *cage is over there.*
We*'re from Bristol.*	***Our*** *Mum is from Bristol, too.*
You*'re new at Cotham School.*	***Your*** *form teacher is Mr Moore.*
They*'re at Imberhorne School.*	***Their*** *school is in East Grinstead.*

Your kann drei verschiedene Bedeutungen haben.

- *I'm* ***your*** *friend, Henry.* — (Ich bin **dein** Freund, Henry.)
- *I'm* ***your*** *English teacher.* — (Ich bin **euer** Englischlehrer.)
- *Is 7DR* ***your*** *form, Mr Robinson?* — (Ist 7DR **Ihre** Klasse, Mr Robinson?)

Vorsicht: ***your*** und ***you're,*** aber auch ***his*** und ***he's, their*** und ***there are*** oder ***it's*** und ***its*** werden leicht miteinander verwechselt. Man muss beim Schreiben deshalb genau aufpassen, welche Form gemeint ist.

your/you're	
Your *pencil case is nice, Susan.*	dein
Your *bags are new, Kevin and Robert.*	euer/eure
Your *form is 7DR, Mr Robinson.*	Ihr
Wow, ***you're*** *great at German, Ben!*	du bist
You're *late, Sheila and Rachel!*	ihr seid
You're *a nice teacher, Mr Miller.*	Sie sind

he's	his
He's *from Bristol.*	***His*** *mother comes from Bristol, too.*

they're	their	there
They're *sisters.*	***Their*** *trousers are very nice.*	***There****'s a mouse on the table.*

it's	its
It's *a beautiful house.*	***Its*** *pencil is on the chair.*

Exercise 1 Find the **possessive determiners** and circle them.

u	g	o	e	j	h	e	r	l	p
p	o	t	h	e	i	r	w	t	q
m	c	e	i	t	s	u	l	s	e
j	i	y	s	d	w	u	y	m	i
l	s	o	p	c	h	e	b	i	a
h	o	u	r	h	e	f	i	l	m
z	u	r	t	e	r	a	s	x	y
h	u	p	q	e	r	t	i	w	s

Exercise 2 Fill in the gaps. Use **my, your, his, her, its, our** or **their.**

David: "This is my sister Patricia. ____________ guinea pig is very clever."

Ethan: "This is my friend Tom. ____________ father is a teacher."

Darren: "Your Mum is very nice, Peter. ____________ Dad is nice, too."

Amy & Fay: "We're in Form 7DR. ____________ teacher is Mr Robinson."

Ronny: "I'm new here. ____________ name is Ronny."

Anil: "Hi, Tim. Hi, Arthur. ____________ cat is very funny."

Peggy: "My friend Amber and my friend Kelly are sisters. ____________ house is in Mansfield Road."

Jack: "Look. This is my tortoise. ____________ cage is in the garden."

Ciara: "Helen is new here. ____________ flat is next to the supermarket."

Kirsten: "Geoffrey and Maurice are friends. ____________ pets Honky and Tonky are very funny."

Exercise 3 Make pairs.

I	*my*	it	____________
____________	your (= *dein*)	____________	their
we	____________	she	____________
he	____________	you (= *Sie*)	____________

Exercise 4 Form sentences.

1 Sarah / school bag – nice *This is Sarah. Her school bag is nice.*

2 Henry / father – teacher *That's Henry.* ____________________

3 Peggy / brother – Form 7RT

____________________.

4 hamster / cage – in the garden

____________________.

5 the Turners / new house – Coventry

These are ____________________.

6 new pupil / chair – over there

____________________.

Exercise 5 **Your** or **you're?** Fill in the gaps. In which cases does **your** have the meaning of *euer?* Circle **your** when it means *euer/eure.*

Mr Miller: "Good morning, boys and girls. I'm ____________ new Maths teacher."

Evelyn: "Our new teacher? But where's Mrs Hunt?"

Mr Miller: "She's ill, I'm afraid."

Ben: "What's ____________ name, sir?"

Mr Miller: "My name is Miller. Mrs Hunt says ____________ a good class."

Alan: "Yes, we're a very good class!"

Mr Miller: "Fine. Take out ____________ folders, please.

Oliver and Nigel come into the classroom."

Mr Miller: "Boys, ____________ late. What are ____________ names?"

Oliver: "I'm Oliver and that's Nigel."

Mr Miller: "OK, sit down, please. Where are we now? Oh, yes, exercise one. Rose, read out ____________ answer, please."

Rose: "It's 36."

Mr Miller: "Great, Rose, ____________ a clever girl."

Rose: "And ____________ a nice teacher, Mr Miller."

Exercise 1

u	g	o	e	j	**h**	**e**	**r**	l	p
p	o	**t**	**h**	**e**	**i**	**r**	w	t	q
m	c	e	**i**	**t**	**s**	u	l	s	e
j	i	**y**	s	d	w	u	y	m	i
l	s	**o**	p	c	h	e	b	i	a
h	**o**	**u**	**r**	h	e	f	i	l	**m**
z	u	**r**	t	e	r	a	s	x	**y**
h	u	p	q	e	r	t	i	w	s

Exercise 2

David: "This is my sister Patricia. **Her** guinea pig is very clever."
Ethan: "This is my friend Tom. **His** father is a teacher."
Darren: "Your Mum is very nice, Peter. **Your** Dad is nice, too."
Amy & Fay: "We're in Form 7DR. **Our** teacher is Mr Robinson."
Ronny: "I'm new here. **My** name is Ronny."
Anil: "Hi, Tim. Hi, Arthur. **Your** cat is very funny."
Peggy: "My friend Amber and my friend Kelly are sisters. **Their** house is in Mansfield Road."
Jack: "Look. This is my tortoise. **Its** cage is in the garden."
Ciara: "Helen is new here. **Her** flat is next to the supermarket."
Kirsten: "Geoffrey and Maurice are friends. **Their** pets Honky and Tonky are very funny."

Exercise 3

I – **my**	it – **its**
you – your (= dein)	**they** – their
we – **our**	she – **her**
he – **his**	you – (= Sie) **your**

Exercise 4

1 This is Sarah. **Her** school bag is nice.
2 That's Henry. **His** father is a teacher.
3 That's Peggy (auch **This is** möglich). **Her** brother is in Form 7RT.
4 This is a hamster. **Its** cage is in the garden.
5 These are the Turners. **Their** new house is in Coventry.
6 This is a new pupil. **His/Her** chair is over there.

Exercise 5

Mr Miller: "Good morning, boys and girls. I'm **your** new maths teacher."
Evelyn: "Our new teacher? But where's Mrs Hunt?"
Mr Miller: "She's ill, I'm afraid."
Ben: "What's **your** name, sir?"
Mr Miller: "My name is Miller. Mrs Hunt says **you're** a good class."
Alan: "Yes, we're a very good class!"
Mr Miller: "Fine. Take out **your** folders, please."
Oliver and Nigel are coming into the classroom.
Mr Miller: "Boys, **you're** late. What are **your** names?"
Oliver: "I'm Oliver and that's Nigel."
Mr Miller: "OK, sit down, please. Where are we now? Oh, yes, exercise one. Rose, read out **your** answer, please."
Rose: "It's 36."
Mr Miller: "Great, Rose, **you're** a clever girl."
Rose: "And **you're** a nice teacher, Mr Miller."

ANSWER KEY ANSWER KEY ANSWER KEY

3 The long and short forms of *to be* (Die Lang- und Kurzformen des Verbs *to be*)

Das englische Verb ***to be*** entspricht dem deutschen Verb *sein*.
Die Form ***to be*** ist der ***to-infinitive*** *(Grundform)*. Die Präsensformen von ***to be*** sind ***am, are, is*** im Singular und ***are*** im Plural.
Sie können als ***long forms*** *(Langformen)* oder als ***short forms*** *(Kurzformen)* verwendet werden.

1 Use

Beim Schreiben verwendet man fast immer die ***long forms.*** Wenn man jedoch spricht, ein Gespräch aufschreibt oder Freunden schreibt, verwendet man meist die ***short forms.*** Bei den Kurzformen wird ein Buchstabe ausgelassen und durch ein Apostroph (') ersetzt.

	long forms		short forms		
singular	*I **am***	*eleven.*	*I'**m***	eleven.	singular
	*You **are***	*funny.*	*You'**re***	funny.	
	*He **is***	*my friend.*	*He'**s***	my friend.	
	*She **is***	*old.*	*She'**s***	old.	
	*It **is***	*a big house.*	*It'**s***	a big house.	
plural	*We **are***	*new here.*	*We'**re***	new here.	plural
	*You **are***	*very nice.*	*You'**re***	very nice.	
	*They **are***	*here.*	*They'**re***	here.	

2 Translations

Aufgepasst bei Übersetzungen! Die englische Wendung ***you are*** kann im Deutschen vier verschiedene Bedeutungen haben.

You are *very nice, Toby.*	Toby, **du bist** sehr nett.
You are *very nice, Mrs Crown.*	Frau Crown, **Sie sind** sehr nett.
You are *very nice, Mr and Mrs Crown.*	Herr und Frau Crown, **Sie sind** sehr nett.
You are *very nice, Toby and Doris.*	Toby und Doris, **ihr seid** sehr nett.

Exercise 1 Find out about Toby. Match the sentences.

Who *is* Mrs Crown?	He *is* Toby's PE teacher.
Who *is* Mr Crown?	Toby: "Yes, I*'m* very happy!"
Where *are* Mr and Mrs Crown?	Mr and Mrs Crown: "We*'re* here!"
Mrs Crown: "Toby, *are* you happy?"	She *is* Toby's classmate.
Mrs Crown makes a joke.	She *is* Toby's German teacher.
Toby: "You*'re* friendly teachers."	They *are* at school.
Doris sits next to Toby in the classroom.	Toby: "You*'re* so funny!"
Toby: "Mr and Mrs Crown, where *are* you?"	Mr and Mrs Crown: "Thanks. You*'re* nice, too."

Exercise 2 Who is in the classroom (= here)? Colour each verb form and match it to the correct personal pronoun or name. Then make sentences as in the example.

They are here.

it | I | you singular | you plural | we | me and Doris | are | am | is | Doris | she | Mr and Mrs Crown | they | Toby | he

Exercise 3 What does Toby **write** and **say?** Fill in the **long forms** and the **short forms** of **to be.**

1 I _______ new here. – Toby: "I_____ new here."

2 You _______ my friend. – Toby: "You___ my friend."

3 Mr Crown _______ a good football player. – Toby: "He___ a good football player."

4 Mrs Crown _______ very good at German. – Toby: "She___ very good at German."

5 Mr and Mrs Crown have got a house. It _______ big. – Toby: "It___ a big house."

6 We _______ new here. – Toby and Doris: "We_____ new here."

7 Mr and Mrs Crown you _______ my teachers. – Toby: "Oh, you_____ my teachers."

8 Mr Crown, you _______ very fast. – Toby: "You_____ very fast."

9 Mr and Mrs Crown _______ old. – Toby: "They_____ old."

Exercise 4 Write sentences with these words. Put the verbs into the correct form.

1 to be / with their friends / at home / Doris and Toby

____.

2 new / this school / I / at / to be

"____."

Exercise 5 Toby is in his German class. Translate the sentences into German for Toby.

1 You're a very good friend, Doris.

____.

2 You're happy teachers, Mr and Mrs Crown.

"____."

3 Mrs Crown, you're the best German teacher in the world.

____.

Exercise 6 Fill in the correct **long forms** or **short forms** of **to be** and the **personal pronouns.**

Doris and Toby ________ very close friends. T________ ________ in the same form. It ________ form 5b. The boys and girls in form 5b ______ happy. Their teacher ________ very nice. Her name _______ Mrs Crown. S________ ________ always fair. Mr Crown _____ her husband. H_____ _______ a teacher, too.

Toby: "Mrs Crown, where __________ you from?"

Mrs Crown: "__________ from Plymouth and Mr Crown __________ from Plymouth, too. __________ both *(= beide)* from Plymouth. __________ a city 190 miles *(= 310 km)* south-west of London."

Toby: "That __________ very interesting. What __________ your hobbies?"

Mrs Crown: "__________ good at playing tennis. __________ have got a lot of *(= viele)* questions. __________ very curious *(= neugierig)!*
What about you, what __________ your hobbies?"

Toby: "Well, __________ lazy *(= faul)*."

Exercise 1

Who **is** Mrs Crown? → She **is** Toby's German teacher.
Who **is** Mr Crown? → He **is** Toby's PE teacher.
Where **are** Mr and Mrs Crown? → They **are** at school.
Mrs Crown: "Toby, **are** you happy?" → Toby: "Yes, I'**m** very happy!"
Mrs Crown makes a joke. → Toby: "You'**re** so funny!"
Toby: "You'**re** friendly teachers." → Mr and Mrs Crown: "Thanks. You're nice, too."
Doris sits next to Toby in the classroom. → She **is** Toby's classmate.
Toby: "Mr and Mrs Crown, where **are** you?" → Mr and Mrs Crown: "We'**re** here!"

Exercise 2

I	→	am	→	here
Toby/he Doris/she it	→	is	→	here
you (singular + plural) Mr and Mrs Crown me and Doris/we	→	are	→	here

Exercise 3

1 I **am** new here. – Toby: "I'**m** new here."
2 You **are** my friend, Doris. – Toby: "You'**re** my friend."
3 Mr Crown **is** a good football player. – Toby: "He'**s** a good football player."
4 Mrs Crown **is** very good at German. – Toby: "She'**s** very good at German."
5 Mr and Mrs Crown have got a house. It **is** big. – Toby: "It'**s** a big house."
6 We **are** new here. – Toby and Doris: "We'**re** new here."
7 Mr and Mrs Crown you **are** my teachers. – Toby: "Oh, you'**re** my teachers."
8 Mr Crown, you **are** very fast. – Toby: "You'**re** very fast."
9 Mr and Mrs Crown **are** old. – Toby: "They'**re** old."

Exercise 4

1 to be/with their friends/at home/Doris and Toby
Doris and Toby are at home with their friends.
2 new / this school/I /at/to be
"I'm new at this school."

Exercise 5

1 You're a very good friend, Doris.
Doris, du bist eine sehr gute Freundin.
2 You're happy teachers, Mr and Mrs Crown.
Herr und Frau Crown, Sie sind glückliche Lehrer.
3 Mrs Crown, you're the best German teacher in the world.
Frau Crown, Sie sind die beste Deutschlehrerin der Welt.

Exercise 6

Doris and Toby **are** very close friends. **They are** in the same form. It **is** form 5b. The boys and girls in form 5b **are** happy. Their teacher **is** very nice. Her name is Mrs Crown. **She is** always fair. Mr Crown **is** her husband. **He is** a teacher, too.

Toby: "Mrs Crown, where **are** you from?"
Mrs Crown: "**I'm** from Plymouth and Mr Crown **is** from Plymouth, too. **We're** both (= beide) from Plymouth. **It's** a city 190 miles (= 310 km) south-west of London."
Toby: "That'**s** very interesting. What **are** your hobbies?"
Mrs Crown: "**I'm** good at playing tennis. **You** have got a lot of (= viele) questions. **You're** very curious (= neugierig)! What about you, what **are** your hobbies?"
Toby: "Well, **I'm** lazy (= faul)."

4 The verb *to be:* negatives and questions with question words (Verneinungen und Fragen mit Fragewörtern des Verbs *to be*)

1 Negative statements with *to be*

Um die Formen von ***to be*** *(sein)* zu verneinen, fügt man hinter dem Verb das Wort ***not*** ein.

	long forms		short forms		
singular	*I **am not***	*eleven.*	*I'**m not***	*eleven.*	singular
	*You **are not***	*nice.*	*You **aren't***	*nice.*	
	*He / She / It **is not***	*old.*	*He / She / It **isn't***	*old.*	
plural	*We **are not***	*stupid.*	*We **aren't***	*stupid.*	plural
	*You **are not***	*in my class.*	*You **aren't***	*in my class.*	
	*They **are not***	*friendly.*	*They **aren't***	*friendly.*	

Bei den ***short forms*** fällt das ***-o*** aus ***not*** weg und wird durch einen Apostroph (') ersetzt. In der 1. Person Singular wird ***not*** nie verkürzt.

2 Questions and short answers with *to be*

Bei Entscheidungsfragen mit dem Verb ***to be*** werden – genauso wie im Deutschen – das ***subject*** und ***verb (to be)*** miteinander vertauscht. Um nicht unhöflich zu sein, antwortet man im Englischen nicht nur mit *Ja / Nein*, sondern (meist) mit einer ***short answer.***

Toby **ist** aus London. *Toby **is** from London.*

Ist Toby aus London? ***Is** Toby from London?*

Ja./Nein. ***Yes, he is./No, he isn't.***

singular	***Am** I clever?*	*Yes, you **are.***	*No, you **aren't.***
	***Are** you nice?*	*Yes, I **am.***	*No, I'**m not.***
	***Is** he/she/it old?*	*Yes, he/she/it **is.***	*No, he/she/it **isn't.***
plural	***Are** we stupid?*	*Yes, we **are.***	*No, we **aren't.***
	***Are** you in my class, Toby and Doris?*	*Yes, we **are.***	*No, we **aren't.***
	***Are** they friendly?*	*Yes, they **are.***	*No, they **aren't.***

In positiven Antworten wird immer die ***long form*** verwendet.
Auf Fragen mit ***Is that ... ?*** wird mit *Yes, **it** is. / No, **it** isn't geantwortet.*
*Is **that Toby?** – Yes, **it** is. / No, **it** isn't.*

3 Questions with question words and *to be*

In Fragen mit ***question words*** *(Fragewörtern)* werden ***subject*** und ***verb*** ebenfalls vertauscht. Das Fragewort steht wie im Deutschen am Anfang. Dabei wird ***is*** häufig verkürzt zu ***'s.***

*Who'**s** your new friend?*
*What'**s** your name?*
*Where **are** you from?*
*How **are** you?*

Exercise 1 What does Toby say? Match the sentences.

I		Monday. There is no school, because it's Sunday.
You		at school. Mr Crown is at home.
He	'm not	at school. Mrs Crown is at home with her husband.
She	isn't	German, I'm British!
It	aren't	in the classroom. Doris and I are in the garden.
We		late for class, Mr and Mrs Crown.
You		sad. Mr and Mrs Crown are very happy in Colchester.
They		unfriendly. You're very polite *(= höflich),* Doris.

Exercise 2 Fill in the correct positive (+) and negative (–) forms of the verb **to be.**

Toby and his friend Doris *are not* (–) at school, they ________ (+) at home in the garden. The garden ________ (+) behind the house. It ________ (–) very big. The house and the garden ________ (–) in London, they ________ (+) in Colchester. Colchester ________ (–) a village, it ________ (+) a city. There ________ (+) many people there, but there ________ (–) many Germans there, because Colchester ________ (–) a German city.

Exercise 3 Toby's questions for you. Fill in short answers.

1 Are you five years old? *No, I* ________.

2 Are you and your friends teachers? ________.

3 Is your school in England? ________.

4 Is your English teacher nice? ________.

5 Toby: Am I a girl? ________.

Exercise 4 Use the information and find the questions to Toby's answers.

Doris: "________?"

Toby: "No, you aren't late for my birthday party."

Doris: "________?"

Toby: "Yes, the birthday cake is very good."

Doris: "________?"

Toby: "No, they aren't. My parents are in the kitchen."

Exercise 5 Toby's pencil case. Fill in the long or short form of **to be.**

Doris: "Toby, where ________ your pencils? They ________ in your pencil case!"

Toby: "That ________ my pencil case! My pencil case ________ over there, in my school bag."

Doris: "Oh, ________ that your pencil case?"

Toby: "Yes, it ________. Open it!"

Doris: "There ________ any pencils in that pencil case."

Toby: "________ you sure?"

Doris: "Yes, I ________. I ________ not stupid!"

Exercise 6 What belongs to Toby? Find the questions and short answers.

1 *Is that Toby's book?* ________________. Yes, ________.

2 ________________. ________.

3 ________________. ________.

4 ________________. ________.

5 ________________. ________.

Exercise 7 Toby's questions for you. Form questions with the words and answer them.

1 Toby: "________________." "I'm ________."

your / what / name / 's?"

2 Toby: "________________." "I'm ________."

are / how / you?"

3 Toby: "________________." "I'm ________."

now / are / where / you?"

Exercise 1

I		Monday. There is no school, because it's Sunday.
You		at school. Mr Crown is at home.
He	'm not	at school. Mrs Crown is at home with her husband.
She	isn't	German, I'm British!
It	aren't	in the classroom. Doris and I are in the garden.
We		late for class, Mr and Mrs Crown.
You		sad. Mr and Mrs Crown are very happy in Colchester.
They		unfriendly. You're very polite (= höflich), Doris.

Exercise 2

Toby and his friend Doris **aren't/are not** (–) at school, they **are** (+) at home in the garden. The garden **is** (+) behind the house. It **isn't/is not** (–) very big. The house and the garden **aren't/are not** (–) in London, they **are** (+) in Colchester. Colchester **isn't/is not** (–) a village, it **is** (+) a city. There **are** (+) many people there, but there **aren't/are not** (–) many Germans there, because Colchester **isn't/is not** (–) a German city.

Exercise 3

1	Are you five years old?	No, I**'m not.**
2	Are you and your friends teachers?	No, **we aren't.**
3	Is your school in England?	No, **it isn't.**
4	Is your English teacher nice?	Yes, **he/she is.**/No, **he/she isn't.**
5	Toby: Am I a girl?	No, **you aren't.**

Exercise 4 Lösungsbeispiele:

Doris: **"Am I late for your birthday party?"**
Toby: "No, you aren't late for my birthday party."
Doris: **"Is the birthday cake good? "**
Toby: "Yes, the birthday cake is very good."
Doris: **"Are your parents in the living room?"**
Toby: "No, they aren't. My parents are in the kitchen."

Exercise 5

Doris: "Toby, where **are** your pencils? They **aren't** in your pencil case!"
Toby: "That **isn't** my pencil case! My pencil case **is** over there, in my school bag."
Doris: "Oh, **is** that your pencil case?"
Toby: "Yes, it **is.** Open it!"
Doris: "There **aren't** any pencils in that pencil case."
Toby: **"Are** you sure?"
Doris: "Yes, I **am.** I'**m** not stupid!"

Exercise 6

1	**Is that Toby's book?**	**Yes, it is.**
2	**Are those Toby's pens?**	**No, they aren't.**
3	**Is that Toby's bike?**	**Yes, it is.**
4	**Are those Toby's shoes?**	**No, they aren't.**
5	**Is that Toby's teacher?**	**Yes, it is.**

Exercise 7 Lösungsbeispiele:

Toby: **"What's your name?"** **"I'm Linda."**

Toby: **"How are you?"** **"I'm fine."**

Toby: **"Where are you now?"** **"I'm from Munich."**

ANSWER KEY ANSWER KEY ANSWER KEY

5 *This/that, these/those* (Demonstrativbegleiter)

Mit den Wörtern ***this/that*** (Singular) und ***these/those*** (Plural) weist man auf etwas hin. Man nennt sie *Demonstrativbegleiter (hinweisende Begleiter).*

1 Singular

this	that
This wird gebraucht, wenn ▪ etwas in der Nähe des Sprechers ist oder ▪ zwei Dinge (oder Personen) vorgestellt werden sollen und es sich um das zuerst genannte handelt.	***That*** wird gebraucht, wenn ▪ sich etwas weiter entfernt befindet oder ▪ zwei Dinge (oder Personen) vorgestellt werden sollen und es sich um das später genannte handelt.
This *picture (here) is funny.* **Dieses** Bild (hier) ist lustig.	***That*** *picture (there) is terrible.* **Das** Bild (da) ist furchtbar.

2 Plural

these	those
These wird gebraucht, wenn ▪ Personen oder Dinge in der Nähe des Sprechers sind oder ▪ zwei Gruppen von Dingen (oder Personen) vorgestellt werden sollen und es sich um die zuerst genannte handelt.	***Those*** wird gebraucht, wenn ▪ sich Personen oder Dinge weiter entfernt befinden oder ▪ zwei Gruppen von Dingen (oder Personen) vorgestellt werden sollen und es sich um die später genannte handelt.
These *school bags (here) are cheap.* **Diese** Schultaschen (hier) sind billig.	***Those*** *school bags (there) are expensive.* **Die** Schultaschen (da) sind teuer.

Wenn ***this/that*** und ***these/those*** nicht vor einem Nomen stehen, sondern anstelle eines Nomens, dann spricht man von Demonstrativpronomen.

Vergleiche: ***This*** *is a good book. (Demonstrativpronomen)*
This *book is good. (Demonstrativbegleiter)*

- Wenn ***that*** als *Demonstrativpronomen* in Verbindung mit ***is*** gebraucht wird, verwendet man beim Sprechen häufig die ***short form*** *(Kurzform)* ***that's.***
  That's *a nice dog.*
- ***That*** und ***those*** als *Demonstrativpronomen* stehen oft zusammen mit ***over there.***
  Those *are my pencils* ***over there.***

Exercise 1 Write sentences. Use **this/that** or **these/those.**

This is a book and that's a CD.

____

____

____

____

____

____

Exercise 2 Write sentences. Use **this is** or **these are.**

This is my school bag.	school bag
______________________	pencil case
______________________	pencils
______________________	pen
______________________	biros
______________________	rubbers
______________________	ruler
______________________	picture of my dog Rufus

Now use **that is** or **those are.**

That is Helen's school bag.	school bag
Those are her English books.	English books
______________________	folders
______________________	German book
______________________	horse magazine
______________________	exercise books
______________________	lunch box
______________________	purse

Exercise 3 Fill in the gaps. Use **this, that, these** and **those.**

Karen: "____________ is a great clothes shop."

Kelly: "Yes, it is. I like the skirts. ____________ skirts are pretty, but ____________ skirts are terrible."

Karen: "Wow, look at ____________ sandals here. They're cheap."

Kelly: "And look at ____________ dress over there. Isn't it pretty?"

Karen: "Yes, it is, but too expensive. What about ____________ dress here?"

Kelly: "No, it's green and I don't like green. But I like _______ shoes in the window."

Karen: "But they're too expensive. What about ____________ shoes here?"

Kelly: "Not bad."

Karen: "But, Kelly, they're green!"

Kelly: "We must go now. Where's my school bag? Is ____ my school bag over there?"

Karen: "No, it isn't. ____________ school bag here is yours."

Exercise 4 Darren and his uncle are looking at the photos on Darren's camera. Choose the right answer and find the secret word. Fill in the letters at the bottom of this text.

1 __________ (This (P)/That (U)) is Henry. He's in my tutor group.

2 __________ (These (H)/Those (G)) boys and girls here are in my tutor group, too.

3 __________ (This (O)/That (E)) man here is Mr Clark. He's my tutor.

4 __________ (This (S)/That (T)) boy over there is Robert.

5 __________ (These (O)/Those (A)) skates here are Robert's skates.

6 __________ (These (U)/Those (A)) skates there are my skates. They're really fast.

7 __________ 's (This (K)/That (L)) great!

8 __________ (This (B)/That (D)) building here is my school. It's a nice school.

9 __________ And look at (this (U)/that (O)) photo here.

10 __________ (These (N)/Those (M)) boys there aren't my friends. My friends are here.

Can you find the secret word?

P	___	___	___	___		___	___	___	___	___
1	2	3	4	5		6	7	8	9	10

Exercise 1

This is a book and that's a CD.

This is a biro and that's a ruler.

These are rubbers and those are pencils.

This is a cat and that's a dog.

This is a window and that's a door.

These are pictures and those are magazines.

Exercise 2

This is my school bag.	school bag
This is my pencil case.	pencil case
These are my pencils.	pencils
This is my pen.	pen
These are my biros.	biros
These are my rubbers.	rubbers
This is my ruler.	ruler
This is a picture of my dog Rufus.	picture of my dog Rufus
That is Helen's school bag.	school bag
Those are her English books.	English books
Those are her folders.	folders
That is her German book.	German book
That is her horse magazine.	horse magazine
Those are her exercise books.	exercise books
That is her lunch box.	lunch box
That is her purse.	purse

Exercise 3

Karen: "**This** is a great clothes shop."

Kelly: "Yes, it is. I like the skirts. **These** skirts are pretty, but **those** skirts are terrible."

Karen: "Wow, look at **these** sandals here. They're cheap."

Kelly: "And look at **that** dress over there. Isn't it pretty?"

Karen: "Yes, it is, but too expensive. What about **this** dress here?"

Kelly: "No, it's green and I don't like green. But I like **those** shoes in the window."

Karen: "But they're too expensive. What about **these** shoes here?

Kelly: "Not bad."

Karen: "But, Kelly, they're green!"

Kelly: "We must go now. Where's my school bag? Is **that** my school bag over there?"

Karen: "No, it isn't. **This** school bag here is yours."

Exercise 4

1 **This** is Henry. He's in my tutor group. 2 **These** boys and girls here are in my tutor group, too. 3 **This** man here is Mr Clark. He's my tutor. 4 **That** boy over there is Robert. 5 **These** skates here are Robert's skates. 6 **Those** skates there are my skates. They're really fast. 7 **That**'s great! 8 **This** building here is my school. It's a nice school. 9 And look at **this** photo here. 10 **Those** boys there aren't my friends. My friends are here.

Can you find the secret word?

P	H	O	T	O	A	L	B	U	M
1	2	3	4	5	6	7	8	9	10

ANSWER KEY ANSWER KEY ANSWER KEY

6 *There is/there are* in statements, negatives and questions (Aussagen, Verneinungen und Fragen mit *there is/there are*)

Wenn man ausdrücken möchte, wo sich ein Gegenstand oder eine Person befindet, bzw. darauf hinweisen will, benutzt man im Englischen ***there is*** bzw. die Kurzform ***there's.*** Handelt es sich um mehrere Dinge oder Personen, verwendet man ***there are.***
Ins Deutsche wird die Singularform ***there is*** mit *da/dort/es ist,* aber auch mit *es gibt* sowie *es/da liegt/steht* oder *es sind* übersetzt. Entsprechend wird die Pluralform ***there are*** mit *es/da/dort sind,* sowie *es gibt* oder *es/da liegen/stehen* übersetzt.

There is *a book on the desk.*	**Da liegt** ein Buch auf dem Tisch. / Auf dem Tisch **liegt** ein Buch.

Beachte die unterschiedlichen Möglichkeiten der Bedeutung im Deutschen:

There are *cats in the park.*	**Da sind** Katzen im Park. (Man weist darauf hin, kann sie sehen.) **Es gibt** Katzen im Park. (Man erzählt davon, ohne sie zu sehen.)

1 Statements of place

Um auszudrücken, wo sich etwas oder jemand befindet, wird der Satz meist mit ***there is*** bzw. ***there are*** eingeleitet und die Ortsangabe steht am Ende des Satzes. Beginnt der Satz mit der Ortsangabe, folgt darauf in der Regel ***there is*** bzw. ***there are,*** und das Objekt steht am Satzende.

There is *a book on the desk.* *On the desk* ***there is*** *a book.*	**Da ist** ein Buch auf dem Tisch. Auf dem Tisch **liegt** ein Buch.
There are *ten girls in our class.* *In our class* ***there are*** *ten girls.*	In unserer Klasse **sind/gibt es** zehn Mädchen.

2 Negative statements

Wenn man sagen will, dass es etwas **nicht** gibt oder dass da etwas **nicht** ist, dann hat man zwei Möglichkeiten: ***there isn't/there is no*** im Singular und ***there aren't/there are no*** im Plural.

There isn't/there is no *a book on the desk.*	Auf dem Tisch **ist/liegt kein** Buch.
In our cooking club ***there aren't*** *any/****there are*** *no boys.*	In unserem Kochclub **gibt es keine** Jungen.

3 Questions and short answers

Wenn man fragen will, ob es etwas/jemanden gibt oder ob da etwas/jemand ist, dann stellt man ***is/are*** nach vorne: ***Is there ...?/Are there ...?*** In der Kurzantwort steht wiederum ***there is/isn't*** bzw. ***there are/aren't.***

Is there *a book on the desk?*	**Ist/liegt auf** dem Tisch ein Buch?	*Yes,* ***there is.***
		No, ***there isn't.***
Are there *any cats in the park?*	**Gibt es** Katzen im Park?	*Yes,* ***there are.***
		No, ***there aren't.***

EXERCISE 1 My big new school. Singular or plural? Fill in the gaps with **is** or **are.**

1 There __________ 1,324 boys and girls at my school.

2 There __________ 36 teachers at my new school.

3 There __________ a new teacher for English at my school. His name is Mr Green.

4 There __________ seven girls in my class. They are nice.

5 There __________ ten boys in my class. They are nice, too.

6 There __________ a boy in my class. His name is Tom. He is my friend.

EXERCISE 2 Look at the picture. Fill in the gaps of the text with **there is** or **there are.**

In the garden ______________________ a big tree. ________________________ a dog and ______________________ two girls and two boys in the garden, too. Under the tree ____________________________ five footballs and five skateboards. In the school bag _____________________ pens and pencils. ____________________ a rubber, too.

EXERCISE 3 Look at the picture again. Fill in these gaps with **there isn't** or **there aren't.**

In the garden ______________________________________ a car. Next to the tree in the garden, ____ a chair. In the school bag _____________________________ any folders and _______________________ a ruler. __________________________ a cat. And _________________________ any beds and __________________________ a desk in the garden – they are in the house, of course!

Exercise 4 Look at the picture on page 33 again and complete the beginnings of the questions with **Is there** or **Are there.** Then answer the questions.

__________ a comic in the garden, too? No, *there isn't.*

__________ any teachers in the garden? No, __________.

They are at school, of course. __________ any flowers in the garden?

Yes, __________. __________ a radio in the garden?

No, __________.

Exercise 5 Write sentences with **There is no** or **There are no.**

1 __________ penguins in Africa.

2 __________ crocodiles in Germany – only in zoos!

3 __________ socks in a pencil case.

4 __________ trees on the moon.

5 __________ alcohol in lemonade.

6 __________ queen or king in Germany – but there is one in England.

7 __________ snow in the summer – but there is often a lot of rain!

Exercise 6 You speak to Sally, an American girl from Washington D. C. What can you say?

Du möchtest wissen, ob es in den USA Krokodile gibt.

You: "__________?"

Sally: "There are crocodiles, but only in the south."

Du sagst, dass es in Deutschland keine Krokodile gibt.

You: "__________."

Sally: "There are no castles in the USA."

Du erzählst, dass es in Deutschland viele Schlösser *(= castles)* gibt.

You: "__________."

Sally: "Is there a ghost in one of them?"

Du antwortest, dass es dort natürlich keinen Geist gibt.

You: "__________."

Exercise 1.

1 There **are** 1,324 boys and girls at my school.
2 There **are** 36 teachers at my new school.
3 There **is** a new teacher for English at my school. His name is Mr Green.
4 There **are** seven girls in my class. They are nice.
5 There **are** ten boys in my class. They are nice, too.
6 There **is** a boy in my class. His name is Tom. He is my friend.

Exercise 2

In the garden **there is** a big tree. **There is** a dog and **there are** two girls and two boys in the garden, too. Under the tree **there are** five footballs and five skateboards. In the school bag **there are** pens and pencils. **There is** a rubber, too.

Exercise 3

In the garden **there isn't** a car. Next to the tree in the garden **there isn't** a chair. In the school bag **there aren't** any folders, **there isn't** a ruler. **There isn't** a cat. **There aren't** any beds and **there isn't** a desk in the garden – they are in the house, of course!

Exercise 4

Is there a comic in the garden, too? No, **there isn't.**
Are there any teachers in the garden? No, **there aren't.**
They are at school, of course.
Are there any flowers in the garden? Yes, **there are.**
Is there a radio in the garden? No, there **isn't.**

Exercise 5

1 **There are no** penguins in Africa.
2 **There are no** crocodiles in Germany – only in zoos!
3 **There are no** socks in a pencil case.
4 **There are no** trees on the moon.
5 **There is no** alcohol in lemonade
6 **There is no** queen or king in Germany – but there is one in England.
7 **There is no** snow in the summer – but there is often a lot of rain!

Exercise 6

Du möchtest wissen, ob es in den USA Krokodile gibt.
You: **"Are there any crocodiles in the USA?"**
Sally: "Yes, there are / There are crocodiles, but only in the south."
Du sagst, dass es in Deutschland keine Krokodile gibt.
You: **"There are no/There aren't any crocodiles in Germany."**
Sally: "There are no castles in the USA."
Du erzählst, dass es in Deutschland viele Schlösser (= castles) gibt.
You: **"There are many castles in Germany."**
Sally: "Is there a ghost in one of them?"
Du antwortest, dass es dort natürlich keinen Geist gibt.
You: **"Of course, there isn't."** Or: **"Of course, there is no ghost/there isn't a ghost."**

Personal pronouns and possessive determiners

Exercise 1 Fill in the missing **personal pronouns.**

subject pronouns		**object pronouns**	
German	English	German	English
ich	________	mir, mich	________
du	________	dir, dich	________
er	________	ihm, ihn	________
sie	________	ihr, sie	________
es	________	ihm, ihn, es	________
wir	________	uns	________
ihr	________	euch	________
sie	________	ihnen, sie	________
Sie	________	Ihnen, Sie	________

18 P

Exercise 2 **Possessive determiners:** Translate into English.

German	English
mein Haus	________
dein Auto	________
sein Mäppchen *(m)*	________
ihr Heft	________
sein Bett *(n)*	________
unser Wohnzimmer	________
euer Essen	________
ihr Wellensittich	________

16 P

Exercise 3 Fill in the missing **personal pronouns** and **possessive determiners.**

Anne is talking to ________ friend Beth: "There are two new girls in ________ class."

Beth: "What are ________ names?"

Anne: "________ names are Lisa and Angela. ________ are from Glasgow."

Beth: “Do ________ like ________ school?”

Anne: “Yes, ________ do. ________ say ________ is a good school. And Lisa likes ______ tutor Mr Smith. ______ says that he is a very nice man and ______ also likes _____ dog. _______ meet in the park every day. Lisa wants to ask ______ if she can go for a walk with ______ dog, too.”

Beth: “Do ________ think that ________ will be ________ friends?”

Anne: “Of course! ________ are very nice and ________ like horses. Like _____. Let ______ ask ________ to play with ________ tomorrow.”

Beth: “Good idea! But _____ ideas are always very good!”

27 P

EXERCISE 4 Listen to the text and then fill in the missing words.

Fred the frog

Fred is a frog. ______ and ______ family live in a park. ______ family is very big: ____ has got five brothers and ten sisters. Allie is ________ favourite sister. ______ is a nice green frog with a beautiful voice. Sometimes __________ sing together. ___________ voices are very loud. This is bad for the Smiths, because _________ house is next to the park where the frogs live. And _________ walls are very thin *(= dünn)*. When Fred and Allie sing, the Smiths cannot sleep. Then Mr Smith says to Mrs Smith: “Why is ____ house so near to the park where all the frogs live? _____’s terrible!” Mrs Smith answers: “Don’t worry, George. ______ don’t have to listen to _______ singing. Go and get ______ favourite CD so that ______ can listen to it.” _______ favourite CD is a CD by Mozart. Mr Smith plays _____ very loud, so the frogs can hear ______, too. ______ think that the music is brilliant. So ______ stop _______ singing and listen to _______. When Mr Smith hears that, _______ is so happy that _______ stops the CD. This makes Fred and Allie so sad that _______ start ______ singing again. Poor Mr Smith.

27 P

EXERCISE 5 Translate into English.

1 Die Katze ist unter dem Schreibtisch. Kannst du sie sehen? ____________________

____

5 P

2 Sie heißt Tinka. Kennst du ihr Lieblingsspiel? ______________________________

____ 5 P

3 Wenn ihre Familie, die Malcolms, Fernsehen schaut, sitzt sie auf dem Wohnzimmertisch. ______________________________

____ 5 P

4 Sie wirft alle Messer und Gabeln vom Tisch. Das macht Spaß! ______________________________

____

____ 7 P

5 Dann ist Herr Malcolm so wütend, dass er seinen Schuh nach ihr wirft. Natürlich trifft er sie nie. ______________________________

____ 8 P

The verb *to be:* long and short forms in questions and answers

Exercise 6 Answer the questions.

1 Are you in class 5a? No, ______________________________.

2 Are we in the same class? Yes, ______________________________.

3 Are these your bags over there? No, ______________________________.

4 Is that your picture? Yes, ______________________________. 8 P

Exercise 7 Fill in the missing words.

1 ____________ your book? Yes, it is. It's very good.

2 ____________ your pencils? No, they aren't. They are Betty's pencils.

3 ____ Evelyn Meyer ____ teacher? Oh yes! And she is my favourite teacher! 6 P

Exercise 8 Ask questions.

1 ______________________________? I'm ten. 2 P

2 ______________________________? I'm fine, thanks. 2 P

3 ______________________________? Yes, it is. His name is Bello. 2 P

4 ______________________________? That is Mr Smith, our tutor. 2 P

This/that, these/those

Exercise 9 Fill in the missing words.

1 Is ________ your English book, Betty? No, my English book is ________ book over there.

2 Are ________ your skates, Alan? No, my skates are ________ on the table.

4 P

There is/there are

Exercise 10 Translate into English.

1 Da ist unser Lehrer Herr Smith.

____.

2 P

2 Und da ist unser Klassenraum.

____.

2 P

3 Es sind drei Schüler im Klassenraum.

____?

3 P

4 Auf dem Tisch liegen drei blaue Stifte.

____.

3 P

5 Und was ist das? Da ist eine Maus auf dem Stuhl, oh je!

____!

4 P

Exercise 11 Anne's room isn't very tidy. Write 10 sentences about Anne's room.

1 ____.

2 ____.

3 ____.

4 ____.

5 ____.

6 ____.

7 ____.

8 ____.

9 ____.

10 ____.

20 P

Mixed bag

EXERCISE 12 Fill in the missing words.

Hello, I _____ Betty Bates. Look, __________ is Lily on ______ skates. Lily is _______ best friend. The skates ________ really fast. ___________ new. Oh no, Lily, _______ ______ hurt? No? ________'s good. And where ______ the new boy from Glasgow? What's __________ name again? Oh yes, William. ________ ______ Tim and John. ___________ in _______ class, too. _________ anoraks look really great. _______ _______ new? And _____ ______ a real BUBA pullover? Wow, _____ looks wonderful! I must get one for myself, too. _____ mother says that I already have many clothes, but I think a girl always needs something new.

22 P

Auswertung Trage rechts deine Gesamtpunktzahl ein und vergleiche.

☺ 200 – 150 points	😐 149 – 100 points	☹ 99 – 0 points

TOTAL SCORE

200

Exercise 1
Subject pronouns: I, you, he, she, it, we, you, they, you
Object pronouns: me, you, him, her, it, us, you, them, you

Exercise 2
my house, your car, his pencil case, her exercise book, its bed, our living room, your food, their/her budgie

Exercise 3
her – my (our) | their | Their | They | they – our (your) | they | They – it | our | She – she – his | They | him – his | you – they – our | They – they | us | us – them – us | your

Exercise 4
He – his | His – he | his | She | they | Their | their | its | our | It | You – their | your – we | His | it – it | They | they – their – it | he – he | they – their

Exercise 5
1 The cat is under the desk. Can you see it?
2 Her name is Tinka. Do you know her favourite game?
3 When her family, the Malcolms, watch TV, she sits on the living room table.
4 She throws all the knives and forks off the table. That is fun!
5 Then Mr Malcolm is so angry that he throws his shoe at her. Of course, he never hits her.

Exercise 6
1 No, **I'm not.** 2 Yes, **we are.**
3 No, **they aren't.** 4 Yes, **it is.**

Exercise 7
1 **Is this (that)** your book?
2 **Are these (those)** your pencils?
3 **Is** Evelyn Meyer **your** teacher?

Exercise 8
1 How old are you?
2 How are you?
3 Is that your dog?
4 Who is that?

Exercise 9
1 Is **this** your English book, Betty? No, my English book is **that** book over there.
2 Are **these** your skates, Alan? No, my skates are **those** on the table.

Exercise 10
1 There is our teacher (tutor) Mr Smith.
2 And there is our classroom.
3 There are three pupils in the classroom.
4 On the table there are three blue pens.
5 And what is that? There is a mouse on the chair, oh dear!

Exercise 11
1 There are two posters on the wall.
2 There is a cat under the bed.
3 There are two mice next to the cat.
4 There are five socks on the bed.
5 There is a laptop on the desk.
6 There is a cake next to the laptop.
7 There is an empty bottle on the desk, too.
8 There are two skates under the desk.
9 There is an anorak on the chair.
10 There are three comics on the chair.

Exercise 12
'm (am) | this (that) – her | my | are | They're | are – you | That | is | his | There – are | They're – my (our) | Their | Are – they | is – this (that) | it | My

7 Prepositions of place and direction (Präpositionen in Orts- und Richtungsangaben)

Präpositionen oder Verhältniswörter geben an, wo sich etwas im Vergleich zu etwas anderem befindet. Sie können sich auf Orts- oder Zeitangaben beziehen.
Die ***prepositions of place*** *(Präpositionen in Ortsangaben)* und ***direction*** *(in Richtungsangaben)* zeigen an, wo sich etwas befindet, oder in welche Richtung sich etwas bewegt.

1 Prepositions of place

Ortsangaben sind z. B. ***in, on, next to, under, behind*** und ***in front of.***

Cecily is ***in*** *the house.*
Cecily ist **im** Haus.

There is a garage ***next to*** *Cecily's house.*
Eine Garage ist **neben** Cecliys Haus.

There is a big tree ***behind*** *Cecily's house.*
Es gibt einen großen Baum **hinter** Cecilys Haus.

Steve is ***on*** *his bed.*
Steve ist **auf** seinem Bett.

Steve's book is ***under*** *his bed.*
Steves Buch ist **unter** seinem Bett.

There is a big box ***in front of*** *Steve's bed.*
Eine große Kiste steht **vor** Steves Bett.

2 Prepositions of direction

Into *(hinein)* und ***onto*** *(hinauf)* geben eine Bewegungsrichtung an. Jemand oder etwas verändert also seine Position und bewegt sich in etwas hinein oder auf etwas hinauf.

Cecily is going ***into*** *the house.*
Cecily geht **ins** Haus **(hinein).**

Steve is jumping ***onto*** *the bed.*
Steve springt **auf** das Bett **(hinauf).**

EXERCISE 1 Chaos in Steve's room. Where is everything? Steve's room isn't very nice. It's very untidy! Now he can't find his things. Can you help him?

1 His chair *is in front of* his desk and the drawer is *next to* his bed, but:

2 his shoe is ______________________________ the drawer.

3 His books are ______________________________ the shelves.

4 His school bag is ______________________________ his toy box.

5 His football is ______________________________.

6 His football poster is ______________________________.

7 The lamp from his desk is ______________________________.

8 His pencil case is ______________________________.

9 His toy cars are ______________________________.

10 His laptop is ______________________________.

11 His pencils are ______________________________.

EXERCISE 2 Make it better. Now Steve's mother is in his room. Steve's mother:
"Oh dear! You must put ...

1 ... your school bag *under the desk*.

2 ... your pencils ______________________________.

3 ... your football ______________________________.

4 ... your toy cars ______________________________, too.

5 ... your football poster ______________________________.

6 ... your lamp ______________________________.

7 ... your books ______________________________.

8 ... your computer ______________________________.

9 ... your pencil case ______________________________."

EXERCISE 3 Oops! Terfel, the little dragon, has got a big box with 20 balls for a game in the classroom. But now the balls are not in the box! Where are they? Make sentences with **there is / there are.**

1 *There is one ball behind* ______________________________ the school bag.

2 *There are two balls* ______________________________ the window.

3 ______________________________ the board.

4 ______________________________ the teacher's desk.

5 ______________________________ the teacher's desk.

6 ______________________________ the chair.

7 ______________________________ the school bag.

8 ______________________________ the pupil's desk.

Exercise 1

1 His chair is **in front of** his desk and the drawer is **next to** his bed, but:
2 his shoe is **in** the drawer.
3 His books are **in front of** the shelves.
4 His school bag is **in** his toy box.
5 His football is **on his bed.**
6 His football poster is **on the floor.**
7 The lamp from his desk is **on his shelf.**
8 His pencil case is **next to his desk.**
9 His toy cars are **on his desk.**
10 His laptop is **under his desk.**
11 His pencils are **under his bed.**

Exercise 2

1 ... your school bag **under the desk.**
2 ... your pencils **into your pencil case.**
3 ... your football **into your toy box.**
4 ... your toy cars **into your toy box,** too.
5 ... your football poster **onto the wall.**
6 ... your lamp **onto your desk.**
7 ... your books **onto your shelves.**
8 ... your computer **onto your desk.**
9 ... your pencil case **into your school bag.**

Steve soll jetzt seine Sachen von einem Ort an einen anderen bewegen, also musst du **into** und **onto** benutzen.

Exercise 3

1 **There is one ball behind** the school bag
2 **There are two balls in front of** the window.
3 **There are two balls in front of** the board.
4 **There are four balls on** the teacher's desk.
5 **There are three balls under** the teacher's desk.
6 **There is one ball on** the chair.
7 **There are three balls in** the school bag.
8 **There are four balls next to** the pupil's desk.

8 Prepositions of time: *at, in, on, after, before* (Präpositionen in Zeitangaben)

Prepositions of time *(Präpositionen in Zeitangaben)* stehen z. B. vor Uhr-, Tages-, oder Jahreszeiten oder in Verbindung mit Wochentagen, Monaten oder Jahreszahlen.

- *I always have a cup of tea* ***at 5 pm.*** – Ich trinke immer um fünf Uhr eine Tasse Tee.
- *Sarah usually goes to the bakery* ***in the mornings.*** – Sarah geht gewöhnlich morgens zum Bäcker.

1 The preposition *at*

At wird mit Uhrzeiten und Ausdrücken verwendet, die eine feste Zeit angeben:

- *We have football practice* ***at 3 o'clock.***
- *Lunch is always* ***at noon.***
- *I am busy* ***at the moment.***

2 The preposition *in*

Das Verhältniswort ***in*** wird bei Angaben zu einer allgemeinen Tageszeit, bei Monaten, Jahreszahlen und Jahreszeiten gebraucht.

in + the +	***morning***	*I drink a glass of milk* ***in the morning.***
	afternoon	*We do our homework* ***in the afternoon.***
	evening	***In the evening,*** *Mr Brown watches sports on TV.*
in	***January***	*My birthday is* ***in January.***
	(the) spring	*Flowers bloom* ***in spring.***
	2008	*My cousin went to South Africa* ***in 2008.***

☞ ***Night*** verlangt meist die Präposition ***at,*** ohne bestimmten Artikel. ***Night*** bedeutet im Englischen nicht nur *Nacht,* sondern auch *Abend: My Mum reads* ***at night.***

3 The preposition *on*

Die Präposition ***on*** wird bei einer näher bestimmten Tageszeit, bei Wochentagen und bei Datumsangaben verwendet.

- ***On Monday,*** *we rode our bikes along the river.*
- ***On Saturday morning,*** *she bought a present for her brother.*
- *Our teacher gave us lots of homework* ***on 1 March.***

4 *After* and *before*

Before *(vor)* und sein Gegenteil ***after*** *(nach)* werden ebenfalls häufig in Zeitangaben gebraucht: *We have breakfast* ***before*** *school. – We have dinner* ***after*** *school.*

☞ Vor ***this/that, every, next, last*** wird keine Präposition verwendet:

- *He called me* ***this*** *morning.*
- *We visit Grandma* ***every*** *Sunday.*
- *They will come back* ***next*** *Friday.*
- *I went to Dublin* ***last*** *September.*

EXERCISE 1 Add **at, in, on** or leave the blank empty if correct.

1 I left school _____ 3 pm.

2 We met Cory in town _____ yesterday.

3 They visited me _____ last Sunday.

4 I have lunch at home _____ Mondays.

5 Austin talked to Kelly _____ Wednesday morning.

6 We went to London _____ June.

7 Did you go to the game _____ 25 February?

8 I bought this skirt _____ the summer.

EXERCISE 2 Say what happens in Nick's family on these days.

Wednesday	Thursday	Friday	Saturday	Sunday

5 pm	7 pm	evening	afternoon	morning

____

____

____

____

____

EXERCISE 3 Add the correct preposition or leave a blank if necessary.

_______________ March, there are lots of storms in this region. A tornado even went through our town _______________ 2011. _______________ Tuesday, we woke up _______________ midnight because our dog started barking. There was a big storm outside. But, _______________ 2 am, the thunderstorm was over, and we went back to bed. Everybody was tired __________ Wednesday morning, but school started __________ 8 am. __________ school, I took a long nap *(= Schläfchen).* My Mum woke me up __________ dinner, and I set the table. I hope we won't get any more storms __________ this spring.

Exercise 4 What can you do when? Match the activities with the times. Then write down your sentences.

- to go to the swimming pool
- to sing Christmas songs
- to look for Easter eggs
- to see the stars
- to build a snowman
- to go to church
- to watch the sun come up

____

____

____

____

____

____

Exercise 5 Translate the sentences below.

1 Sonntags stehe ich nie vor 9 Uhr auf.

______________________________.

2 Nick hat 2007 seine Familie in Deutschland besucht.

______________________________.

3 Nach dem Mittagessen haben wir Englisch. Um 14:00 Uhr gehen wir in den Musiksaal.

______________________________.

Exercise 1

1 I left school **at** 3 pm.
2 We met Cory in town yesterday.
3 They visited me last Sunday.
4 I have lunch at home **on** Mondays.
5 Austin talked to Kelly **on** Wednesday morning.
6 We went to London **in** June.
7 Did you go to the game **on** 25 February?
8 I bought this skirt **in** the summer.

Exercise 2

Wednesday	Thursday	Friday	Saturday	Sunday

5 pm	7 pm	evening	afternoon	morning

Nick has football practice **at 5 pm on Wednesdays.**
Nick's father comes back from work **at 7 pm on Thursdays.**
On Friday evenings, Nick's family goes to the cinema.
On Saturday afternoons, Nick plays the guitar.
On Sunday mornings, the family has a big breakfast together.

Exercise 3

In March, there are lots of storms in this region. A tornado even went through our town **in 2011. On Tuesday,** we woke up **at midnight** because our dog started barking. There was a big storm outside. But, **at 2 am,** the thunderstorm was over, and we went back to bed. Everybody was tired **on Wednesday morning,** but school started **at 8 am. After school,** I took a long nap (= Schläfchen). My Mum woke me up **before dinner,** and I set the table. I hope we won't get any more storms **this spring.**

Exercise 4

- to go to the swimming pool
- to sing Christmas songs
- to look for Easter eggs
- to see the stars
- to build a snowman
- to go to church
- to watch the sun come up

December winter night morning summer April Sundays

I can go to the swimming pool **in the summer.**
I sing Christmas songs **in December.**
I look for Easter eggs **in April.**
I see the stars **at night.**
I can build a snowman **in winter.**
I go to church **on Sundays.**
I can watch the sun come up **in the morning.**

Exercise 5

1 Sonntags stehe ich nie vor 9 Uhr auf.
On Sundays, I never get up before 9 am.
2 Nick hat 2007 seine Familie in Deutschland besucht.
Nick visited his family in Germany in 2007.
3 Nach dem Mittagessen haben wir Englisch. Um 14 Uhr gehen wir in den Musiksaal.
After lunch, we have English. At 2 pm, we go to the music room.

ANSWER KEY ANSWER KEY ANSWER KEY

9 Nouns and their plural forms: regular and irregular (Nomen: regelmäßige und unregelmäßige Pluralformen)

1 Nouns: regular plural forms

Die meisten ***nouns*** *(Nomen)* im Englischen bilden ihren Plural regelmäßig, indem man ein ***-(e)s*** an den Singular anhängt.

- *book - book**s***
- *idea - idea**s***
- *class - class**es***
- *pencil case - pencil cas**es***

Vorsicht bei der Aussprache:

[s] (scharfes s)	[z] (weiches s)	[ɪz]
*two boo**ks*** [ks] *four ca**ts*** [ts]	*ten id**eas*** [z] *two frie**nds*** [dz]	*two pencil ca**ses*** [sɪz] *three senten**ces*** [sɪz]
Nach den stimmlosen Konsonanten [p, t, k, f, θ] wird -[s] gesprochen.	Nach Vokalen und den stimmhaften Konsonanten [b, d, g, l, m, n, ð, v] wird -[z] gesprochen.	Nach den Zischlauten [s, z, ʃ, tʃ, ʒ, dʒ] wird -[ɪz] gesprochen. Die Schreibung lautet hier immer ***-es,*** so muss manchmal ein ***e*** eingefügt werden.

2 Nouns: irregular plural forms

Einige ***nouns*** bilden ihren Plural unregelmäßig.

nouns, die auf ***-f(e)*** enden	***nouns,*** die auf ***Konsonant + y*** enden	***nouns*** mit einem völlig unregelmäßigen Plural
*shel**f*** [-f] - *shel**ves*** [-vz] *thie**f*** - *thie**ves*** Das ***-f*** am Wortende wird im Plural also zu ***-ves.***	*fami**ly*** - *fami**lies*** *hob**by*** - *hob**bies*** Das ***-y*** am Wortende wird im Plural also zu ***-ies.***	*m**a**n* [æ] - *m**e**n* [e] *w**o**man* ['wʊmən] - *w**o**men* ['wɪmɪn] *ch**i**ld* [tʃaɪld] - *ch**i**ld**ren*** ['tʃɪldrən] *f**oo**t* [ʊ] - *f**ee**t* [iː] *t**oo**th* [uː] - *t**ee**th* [iː] *m**ouse*** [aʊ] - *m**ice*** [aɪ] *fish - fish* *sheep - sheep* *person - people* **Merke:** *people (= Leute)* gibt es nur im Plural, der Singular heißt *person.*

- Nomen, die auf **Vokal + y** enden, bilden ihren Plural regelmäßig: *bo**y*** - *bo**ys***
- Nomen mit einem unregelmäßigen Plural bilden den ***s-genitive*** durch Anhängen eines ***'s***: *The women**'s** skirts are nice.*

EXERCISE 1 Underline the **nouns** and write them down with their singular and plural form.

old | house | father | cat | green | be | pet | pencil

have | new | school | pen | funny | biro

house – *houses* ______ – ______

______ – ______ ______ – ______

______ – ______ ______ – ______

______ – ______ ______ – ______

______ – ______ ______ – ______

EXERCISE 2 Put these plural words in the right lists. Be careful with the pronunciation.

cats | pencil cases | books | biros | exercises | friends | teachers

watches | schools | bags | colours | tutors | sentences | skirts

sounds | dresses | shirts | desks

[s] (scharfes s)	[z] (weiches s)	[ɪz]
cats		

EXERCISE 3 Irregular plural forms. Can you find the right **nouns?** Write down the singular and the plural forms.

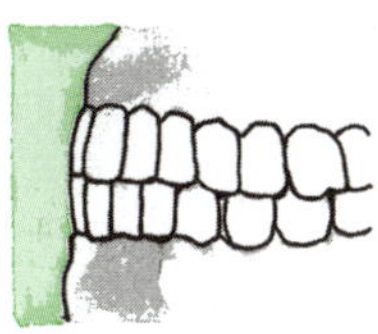

foot – feet ______ ______ ______

______________ ______________ ______________

Exercise 4 Write the plural forms.

box – *boxes*	sister – ______
card – *cards*	mother – ______
girl – ______	sweatshirt – ______
boy – ______	hamster – ______
hobby – ______	bookshelf – ______
brother – ______	cupboard – ______
knife – ______	film – ______
class – ______	child – ______
family – ______	party – ______
present – ______	tutor group – ______

Some words have irregular plural forms. Underline them with a pen.

Exercise 5 Irregular plural or ***-(e)s***? Fill in the gaps.

This is my brother Ben. I have two brother___ and two sister___. Together there are five child___. With our mother and father there are seven people___ in our family. Ben has two hamster___ and three (mouse)________. My sister Sheila has two dog___ and four cat___. So we have a lot of pet___ in our family. But we don't have animal___ like cow___ or horse___. Other famil(y)___ have lots of pet___, too. The Watsons, for example, have five guinea pig___. Their name___ are Molly, Dolly, Ruby, Lucy and Toby.

Exercise 1

old, house, father, cat, green, be, pet, pencil, have, new, school, pen, funny, biro

house – houses
father – fathers
cat – cats
pet – pets
pencil – pencils
school – schools
pen – pens
biro – biros

woman – women

child – children

man – men

Ausnahmen: belief – belief**s**, computer mouse – computer **mouses**

Exercise 2

[s]	[z]	[ɪz]
cats	biros	pencil cases
books	friends	exercises
shirts	teachers	watches
skirts	schools	sentences
desks	bags	dresses
	colours	
	tutors	
	sounds	

Exercise 3

foot – feet

shelf – shelves

mouse – mice

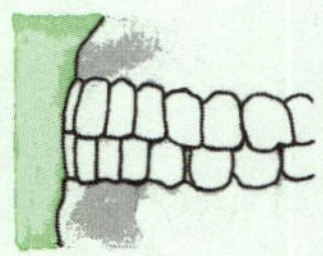

tooth – teeth

Exercise 4

box	– boxes	sister	– sisters
card	– cards	mother	– mothers
girl	– girls	sweatshirt	– sweatshirts
boy	– boys **(Merke: Vokal + *y*)**	hamster	– hamsters
hobby	– hobbies	bookshelf	– bookshelves
brother	– brothers	cupboard	– cupboards
knife	– knives **(Merke: Nomen + *-f(e)*)**	film	– films
class	– classes	child	– children
family	– families	party	– parties
present	– presents	tutor group	– tutor groups

Exercise 5

This is my brother Ben. I have two brother**s** and two sister**s**. Together there are five child**ren**. With our mother and father there are seven **people** in our family. Ben has two hamster**s** and three (mouse) **mice**. My sister Sheila has two dog**s** and four cat**s**. So we have a lot of pet**s** in our family. But we don't have animal**s** like cow**s** or horse**s**. Other famil**ies** have lots of pet**s**, too. The Watsons, for example, have five guinea pig**s**. Their name**s** are Molly, Dolly, Ruby, Lucy and Toby.

10 Short answers with forms of *to be* (Kurzantworten mit *to be*)

Short answers *(Kurzantworten)* mit ***to be*** werden meistens nach Entscheidungsfragen (Fragen, auf die die Antwort ***Yes*** oder ***No*** lauten kann) benutzt, um eine knappe Antwort zu geben. Durch eine Kurzantwort mit ***to be*** wird entweder bestätigt, dass etwas tatsächlich so wie in der Frage bzw. Aussage ist. Oder man stellt klar, dass es nicht so ist:

I	*Yes, I am.*	*No, I am not.* *No, I'm not.*	*we*	*Yes, we are.*	*No, we are not.* *No, we aren't.*
you	*Yes, you are.*	*No, you are not.* *No, you aren't.*	*you*	*Yes, you are.*	*No, you are not.* *No, you aren't.*
he *she* *it*	*Yes, he is.* *Yes, she is.* *Yes, it is.*	*No, he is not.* *No, he isn't.* *No, she is not.* *No, she isn't.* *No, it is not.* *No, it isn't.*	*they*	*Yes, they are.*	*No, they are not.* *No, they aren't.*

1 Short answers with *No*

Die ***short forms*** von ***to be*** können nur bei ***short answers*** mit ***No*** verwendet werden.

Are you two years old?	*No, I'm not.*

Eine ***short answer*** ist im Englischen schon ein ganzer Satz. Aber natürlich kann man noch einen weiteren Satz anfügen, um mehr Informationen zu geben.

Is Mr Johnson a terrible teacher?	*No, he isn't. He's a very nice teacher.*

Nur mit ***Yes*** oder nur mit ***No*** zu antworten, klingt im Englischen unhöflich und ist keine ausreichende Antwort.

2 Short answers with *Yes*

Kurzantworten mit ***Yes*** können nicht abgekürzt werden. Es wird immer die ***long form*** *(Langform)* verwendet.

Are you German?	*Yes, I am.*

Mit ***Yes*** kann man auch sagen, dass eine Aussage falsch ist. Die bejahte Kurzantwort bedeutet dann: „Doch!"

Dirk Nowitzki isn't a good basketball player.	*Yes, he is.*
Dirk Nowitzki ist kein guter Basketball-Spieler.	*Doch!*

3 Short answers with *there is / there are*

Auf eine Frage mit ***there is/there are*** antwortet man mit ***there is(n't)/there are(n't).***

Is there a ball on the table?	*No, there isn't. There's a pen on the table.*
Are there 25 pupils in the classroom?	*Yes, there are.*

EXERCISE 1 Complete these **short answers** with the right forms.

1 Is your school nice? Yes, *it is* ______________________
2 Is Mr Miller a woman? No, ______________________.
3 Is Terfel a nice dragon? Yes, ______________________.
4 Are you a teacher? No, ______________________.
5 Are your friends pupils? Yes, ______________________.
6 Is your mother four years old? No, ______________________.
7 Are you and your friends at one school? Yes, ______________________.
8 Are you a girl? ______________________.

EXERCISE 2 Look at the picture and give the right **short answers.**

1 Is the sun in the sky? *Yes, it is.* ______________________.
2 Is the rabbit next to the sun? ______________________.
3 Are there two children in the picture? ______________________.
4 Is Terfel under the tree? ______________________.
5 Is the bird in the tree? ______________________.
6 Are all the apples in the tree? ______________________.
7 Is Cecily smiling? ______________________.
8 Are the flowers behind the bush? ______________________.

Exercise 3 It's all wrong! Use **short answers** to say that the statements aren't right. Use the **short form** if possible.

1 The *Mona Lisa* isn't a good painting. *Yes, it is!*

2 Peter's dog is green. ______!

3 Cecily and Steve aren't children. ______!

4 A lot of horses are pink. ______!

5 Yellow isn't one of the colours of the rainbow. ______!

6 Our eyes aren't important. ______!

7 School is always terrible. ______!

8 We aren't pupils. ______!

9 You are a boy with pink hair. ______!

Exercise 4 You are Steve. Give **short answers.** They can be positive (☺) or negative (☹). Use the **short form** if possible.

Terfel: Steve:

1 Hi, Steve. Am I your best friend? ☺ ______.

2 Are we in class 5c? ☹ ______.

3 Are your parents in their shop? ☺ ______.

4 Is our English teacher a man? ☹ ______.

5 Are you at kindergarten? ☹ ______.

6 Is your friend Cecily nice? ☺ ______.

7 Are her school things in her room? ☺ ______.

8 Is your house in Park Street? ☹ ______.

9 Are you in a football team? ☺ ______.

10 But you aren't a good player! ☺ ______!

11 Are you good at basketball? ☹ ______.

12 And you are a bad piano player! ☹ ______!

Exercise 1

1 Is your school nice? **Yes, it is.**
2 Is Mr Miller a woman? **No, he is not. / No, he isn't.**
3 Is Terfel a nice dragon? **Yes, he is.**
4 Are you a teacher? **No, I am not. / No, I'm not.**
5 Are your friends pupils? **Yes, they are.**
6 Is your mother four years old? **No, she is not. / No, she isn't.**
7 Are you and your friends at one school? **Yes, we are.**
8 Are you a girl? **Yes, I am. / No, I am not. / No, I'm not.**

Exercise 2

1 Is the sun in the sky? **Yes, it is.**
2 Is the rabbit next to the sun? **No, it is not./No, it isn't.**
3 Are there two children in the picture? **No, there are not./No, there aren't.**
4 Is Terfel under the tree? **No, he is not./No, he isn't.**
5 Is the bird in the tree? **Yes, it is.**
6 Are all the apples in the tree? **No, they are not./No, they aren't.**
7 Is Cecily smiling? **Yes, she is.**
8 Are the flowers behind the bush? **No, they are not./No, they aren't.**

Exercise 3

1 The *Mona Lisa* isn't a good painting. **Yes, it is!**
2 Peter's dog is green. **No, it isn't!**
3 Cecily and Steve aren't children. **Yes, they are!**
4 A lot of horses are pink. **No, they aren't!**
5 Yellow isn't one of the colours of the rainbow. **Yes, it is!**
6 Our eyes aren't important. **Yes, they are!**
7 School is always terrible. **No, it isn't!**
8 We aren't pupils. **Yes, we are!**
9 You are a boy with pink hair. **No, I'm not!**

Exercise 4

	Terfel:		Steve:
1	Hi, Steve. Am I your best friend?	☺	**Yes, you are.**
2	Are we in class 5c?	☹	**No, we aren't.**
3	Are your parents in their shop?	☺	**Yes, they are.**
4	Is our English teacher a man?	☹	**No, she isn't.**
5	Are you at kindergarten?	☹	**No, I'm not.**
6	Is your friend Cecily nice?	☺	**Yes, she is.**
7	Are her school things in her room?	☺	**Yes, they are.**
8	Is your house in Park Street?	☹	**No, it isn't.**
9	Are you in a football team?	☺	**Yes, I am.**
10	But you aren't a good player!	☺	**Yes, I am!**
11	Are you good at basketball?	☹	**No, I'm not.**
12	And you are a bad piano player!	☹	**No, I'm not!**

11 The imperative (Der Imperativ)

1 The imperative: positive form

Wenn man möchte, dass jemand etwas tut oder dass etwas geschieht, dann verwendet man den ***imperative*** *(Befehlsform)*. Wie im Deutschen benutzt man bei der Befehlsform in der 2. Person Singular kein Pronomen. Damit der ***imperative*** freundlich und nicht unhöflich klingt, fügt man im Englischen meist ***please*** ein. Beim ***imperative*** ist es egal, ob eine oder mehrere Personen angesprochen werden, die Form ist immer gleich (wie der Infinitiv des Verbs ohne ***to***).

Im Englischen wird bei einem Befehl kein Ausrufezeichen, sondern eher ein Punkt gesetzt. Das Verb steht immer am Anfang.

statement		→	imperative	
I	*close*	*the door.*	***Close***	*the door, please.*
You	*can go*	*home.*	***Go***	*home, please.*
We	*turn*	*around.*	***Turn***	*around, please.*
You	*must watch*	*those videos.*	***Watch***	*those videos.*

Mit dem ***imperative*** kann man nicht nur Befehle und Anweisungen ausdrücken. Er wird auch für Ratschläge verwendet:

- ***Tell*** *him about your problems. He can help you.*

Außerdem findet man ihn auf Hinweisschildern (z. B. an Türen):

- ***Push / Pull***

Er wird ebenso für höfliche Aufforderungen verwendet:

- *Please* ***sit*** *down and* ***have*** *a piece of cake.*

Eine Aufforderung oder Einladung klingt besonders höflich, wenn das Hilfsverb ***to do*** im Imperativ steht.

- ***Do*** *come, please. /* ***Do*** *sit down, please. /* ***Do*** *be quiet, please.*

2 The imperative: negative form

Wenn man jemandem etwas verbieten möchte, dann verwendet man die ***negative form*** des ***imperative*** *(verneinte Befehlsform)*. Auch der verneinte Imperativ ist in allen Formen gleich. Er setzt sich zusammen aus ***don't*** und dem Vollverb ohne ***to.***

statement			imperative	
You	*should* (= solltest) *not turn*	*left.*	***Don't turn***	*left.*
He	*must not write*	*on the table.*	***Don't write***	*on the table.*
We	*must not sing*	*too loud.*	***Don't sing***	*too loud, please.*
They	*should* (= sollten) *not go*	*home.*	***Don't go***	*home.*

EXERCISE 1 Match:

1	Stay behind the	a)	about her.
2	Tell me all	b)	the door, please.
3	Shut	c)	into my room.
4	Take your feet off	d)	line, please.
5	Don't come	e)	the table.

EXERCISE 2 Jenny has made some rules *(= Regeln)* for her room. Translate the following sentences:

1 Komm nicht in mein Zimmer, bevor ich „Komm rein!" sage. ______________________________.

2 Sprich nicht zu laut! ______________________________.

3 Bring mir ein Geschenk mit. ______________________________.

4 Sag auch zu meiner Katze „Hallo!". ______________________________.

5 Bitte füttere meine Katze nicht! ______________________________.

6 Setz dich nicht auf mein Bett! ______________________________.

7 Setz dich auf den Stuhl vor meinem Schreibtisch. ______________________________.

8 Lege deine Füße nicht auf meinen Schreibtisch! ______________________________.

9 Höre nur Musik, die mir auch gefällt. ______________________________.

10 Rühr nichts an! ______________________________.

11 Öffne nicht das Fenster. ______________________________.

Exercise 3 A tourist asks Jenny the way to the cinema. Jenny tells him. Write down the missing words.

Tourist: "________________ (Entschuldigen Sie) me, can you tell me the way to the cinema, ______________ (bitte)?"

Jenny: "Of course, that's easy. ________________ (Geben Sie) me your map, please. ____________ (Gehen Sie) down Smithy Row. ________________ (Biegen Sie) left into Long Row. _______________________ (Gehen Sie) down Long Row. ___________________________________ (Gehen Sie nicht) into Blue Road. _______________________ (Biegen Sie) right into Red Lane. ____________ (Gehen Sie) down Red Lane and the cinema is on your left."

Tourist: "Thank you very much!"

Jenny: "You're welcome. _______________________ (Haben Sie) a nice day!"

Exercise 4 Finish this letter. Use these the following verbs.

to be · to come · to drive · to feel · to forget · to make · to open

to see · to take · to turn · to wait

Sometimes you need the **negative form.**

Dear Anne,

_______________ and _____________ me next weekend. I live in a house near the mountains. ______________________________ to bring a warm anorak with you. It is cold in the evenings.

It is not difficult to find my house. When you come to the church, ________________ left and _____________ to the end of the road.

___________________ careful, it is a dangerous road. If I am not at home when you arrive, ___________________________________ for me!

_____________________ the key from under the door mat and _____________________ the door. ___________________ yourself something to eat and ______________ at home.

See you soon,

Lily

Exercise 1

1 Stay behind the	a) about her.
2 Tell me all	b) the door, please.
3 Shut	c) into my room.
4 Take your feet off	d) line, please
5 Don't come	e) the table.

Exercise 2

1 Komm nicht in mein Zimmer, bevor ich „Komm rein!“ sage.
Don't come into my room before I say 'Come in'!

2 Sprich nicht zu laut!
Don't talk too loud.

3 Bring mir ein Geschenk mit.
Bring me a present.

4 Sag auch zu meiner Katze „Hallo!“.
Say 'Hello!' to my cat, too.

5 Bitte füttere meine Katze nicht!
Please don't feed my cat.

6 Setz dich nicht auf mein Bett!
Don't sit on my bed.

7 Setz dich auf den Stuhl vor meinem Schreibtisch.
Sit on the chair in front of my desk.

8 Lege deine Füße nicht auf meinen Schreibtisch!
Don't put your feet on my desk.

9 Höre nur Musik die mir auch gefällt.
Only listen to music that I like, too.

10 Rühr nichts an!
Don't touch anything.

11 Öffne nicht das Fenster.
Don't open the window.

Exercise 3

Tourist: "**Excuse** me, can you tell me the way to the cinema, **please?"**

Jenny: "Of course, that's easy. **Give** me your map, please. **Go** down Smithy Row. **Turn** left into Long Row. **Go** down Long Row. **Don't go** into Blue Road. **Turn** right into Red Lane. **Go** down Red Lane and the cinema is on your left."

Tourist: "Thank you very much!"

Jenny: "You're welcome. **Have** a nice day!"

Exercise 4

to be | to come | to drive | to feel | to forget | to make
to open | to see | to take | to turn | to wait

Dear Anne,

Come and **see** me next weekend. I live in a house near the mountains. **Don't forget** to bring a warm anorak with you. It is cold in the evenings.
It is not difficult to find my house. When you come to the church, **turn** left and **drive** to the end of the road. **Be** careful, it is a dangerous road. If I am not at home when you arrive, **don't wait** for me! **Take** the key from under the door mat and **open** the door. **Make** yourself something to eat and **feel** at home.

See you soon,
Lily

12 Genitive expressions: the *s*- and the *of-genitive* (Der Genitiv mit *s* und *of*)

Der Genitiv eines Nomens drückt aus, dass einer Person oder einem Tier etwas gehört. Auch Dingen können andere Dinge zugeordnet sein. Man kann den Genitiv mit ***whose*** *(wessen)* erfragen.
Der ***s-genitive*** *(Genitiv mit s)* wird meist für Personen und Tiere, der ***of-genitive*** *(Genitiv mit of)* für Gegenstände verwendet.

1 The *s-genitive*

Im Singular werden, anders als im Deutschen, Apostroph **(')** und ***s*** an das Nomen angehängt ('s).

singular	
*This is Jack**'s** bike and those are Alice**'s** new skates over there.*	Dies ist Jack**s** Fahrrad und das dort drüben sind Alice**s** neue Rollschuhe.
*The cat**'s** bed is in the kitchen.*	Das Bett **der** Katze ist in der Küche.

Bei regelmäßigen Pluralformen, die auf ***-s*** enden, wird nur ein Apostroph **(')** an das Nomen angehängt.

plural	
*These are my friend**s'** bikes.*	*The cat**s'** toys are in the house.*

*The cat**'s** bed is in the kitchen.* *The cat**s'** toys are in the house.*

Bei unregelmäßigen Pluralformen, die nicht auf ***-s*** enden, wird wie beim Singular ein Apostroph **(')** ***-s*** an das Nomen angefügt.

- *Our children**'s** friends are in the living room.*
- *Women**'s** skirts are really too short today.*

2 The *of-genitive*

Man verwendet den ***of-genitive*** für Gegenstände und abstrakte Nomen wie z. B. Farben, Tage, Orte etc.

- *In the centre **of London** you can visit the Tower.*
- *The windows **of my house** are white.*
- *Monday is the first day **of our school week.***

Exercise 1 Which form is correct: **'s** or **s'?** Underline it.

Anna Webb is my best friend. *Anna's/Annas'* house is in Newcastle. The *Webb's/Webbs'* pet is a very big black and white cat. The *cat's/cats'* bed is in their kitchen. The Webbs have got lots of neighbours. Their *neighbour's/neighbours'* houses are next to their house. *Mr Webb's/Mr Webbs'* office is in Newcastle, too.

Exercise 2 Singular and plural forms. Put in **'s** or **s'.**

The teachers at Anna____ school are usually very nice. Her Maths teacher____ name is Mr Wong. His father____ father came from Asia. There are 25 pupils in her class. With all the pupil____ chairs and desks in their classroom, it gets very full. The children____ ages are 11 or 12. Mr Wong____ favourite pupils are those who are good at Maths. They all wear school uniform. The girl____ skirts are dark blue and the boy____ trousers are blue, too, of course.

Exercise 3 Write down correct **of-genitives** with the words on the left.

house / roof	*the roof of the house*
name / my street	____________________
my sister's hair / colour	____________________
song / the beginning	____________________
end / the night	____________________
Newcastle / city centre	____________________
size / my friend's room	____________________
this word / first letter	____________________

Exercise 4 The **of-genitive.** Write down sentences with these words.

1 of / Anna / is / Newcastle / in the old town / going shopping

____.

2 But / her favourite CD / the price / too high / is / of

____.

3 this band / of / The name / "Nonames" / is

____.

Exercise 5 Put in the right form of the words in brackets: **s** or **of-genitive.**

Anna Webb has got a little brother. ____________________ (name / her brother) is Kevin, and he is six. He goes to a primary school in a ____________________ (suburb / Newcastle). The ____________________ (his school / name) is "South Gosforth".

Today they are learning the ____________________ (the alphabet / second letter). ____________________ (teachers / Kevin) are very happy with him. He has got lots of friends in his class. ____________________ (his friends / favourite game) is football. They play football at ____________________ (every lunch break / the beginning). Then they have lunch. ____________________ (the children / favourite dish) is pizza.

Exercise 6 Be careful: **s** or **of-genitive** or **plural?** Use these words:

name of the football club | number of people | his children's | famous bridges | team's | shops | Mr Webb's | Webbs | part of Newcastle | people

The Webb family and Newcastle

The ____________ are a family from Newcastle. Their house is in a ____________________ which is north of the city centre. Its name is "Gosforth". The ____________________ living in Newcastle is about 271,000. There are many ____________ in the city centre and some ____________________ across the river "Tyne". "Newcastle United" is the ____________________. Lots of ____________ go to the matches every weekend. The colours of the ____________ football shirts are black, white and orange. Anna's dad likes football, too. ____________ next birthday present is a ticket for the football match against Liverpool – ____________ idea.

Exercise 1

Anna Webb is my best friend. **Anna's / Annas'** house is in Newcastle. The **Webb's / Webbs'** pet is a very big black and white cat. The **cat's / cats'** bed is in their kitchen. The Webbs have got lots of neighbours. Their **neighbour's/ neighbours'** houses are next to their house. **Mr Webb's / Mr Webbs** office is in Newcastle, too.

Exercise 2

The teachers at **Anna's** school are usually very nice. Her Maths **teacher's** name is Mr Wong. His **father's** father came from Asia. There are 25 pupils in her class. With all the **pupils'** chairs and desks in their classroom, it gets very full. The **children's** ages are 11 or 12. Mr **Wong's** favourite pupils are those who are good at Maths. They all wear school uniform. The **girls'** skirts are dark blue and the **boys'** trousers are blue, too, of course.

Exercise 3

house / roof	**the roof of the house**
name / my street	**the name of my street**
my sister's hair / colour	**the colour of my sister's hair**
song / the beginning	**the beginning of this song**
end / the night	**the end of the night**
Newcastle / city centre	**the city centre of Newcastle**
size / my friend's room	**the size of my friend's room**
this word / first letter	**the first letter of this word**

Exercise 4

1 Anna is going shopping in the old town of Newcastle.
2 But the price of her favourite CD is too high.
3 The name of this band is "Nonames".

Exercise 5

Anna Webb has got a little brother.
Her brother's name is Kevin, and he is six.
He goes to a primary school in a **suburb of Newcastle.**
The name of his school is "South Gosforth".
Today they are learning the **second letter of the alphabet.**
Kevin's teachers are very happy with him.
He has got lots of friends in his class.
His friends' favourite game is football.
They play football at **the beginning of every lunch break.**
Then they have lunch. **The children's favourite dish** is pizza.

Exercise 6

name of the football club | number of people | his children's | famous bridges | team's | shops | Mr Webb's | Webbs | part of Newcastle | people

The Webbs are a family from Newcastle.
Their house is in a **part of Newcastle** which is north of the city centre. Its name is "Gosforth".
The **number of people** living in Newcastle is about 271,000.
There are many **shops** in the city centre and some **famous bridges** across the river "Tyne".
"Newcastle United" is the **name of the football club.**
Lots of **people** go to the matches every weekend.
The colours of the **team's** football shirts are black, white and orange.
Anna's dad likes football, too.
Mr Webb's next birthday present is a ticket for the football match against Liverpool – **his children's** idea.

ANSWER KEY ANSWER KEY ANSWER KEY

13 *Have got* (Besitz ausdrücken mit *have got*)

Have got/has got bedeutet im Deutschen *haben* oder *besitzen*. In der 3. Person Singular ***(he, she, it)*** verwendet man ***has got***, in allen anderen Personen ***(I, you, we, they)*** verwendet man ***have got.***

1 Long and short forms of *have got*

Die ***long forms*** *(Langformen)* werden eher in der geschriebenen Sprache, die ***short forms*** *(Kurzformen)* überwiegend in der gesprochenen Sprache benutzt. Bei den ***short forms*** werden die ersten beiden Buchstaben von ***have /has*** weggelassen und durch ein Auslassungszeichen, den Apostroph ('), ersetzt.

long forms	short forms
*I **have got** a nice house.*	*I**'ve got** a nice house.*
*You **have got** two sisters.*	*You**'ve got** two sisters.*
*He / She / It **has got** a big room.*	*He**'s** / She**'s** / It**'s got** a big room.*
*We **have got** two cats.*	*We**'ve got** two cats.*
*You **have got** good marks.*	*You**'ve got** good marks.*
*They **have got** a very small classroom.*	*They**'ve got** a very small classroom.*

2 Short forms of *have got* with pronouns

In der Regel werden die ***short forms*** bei den ***pronouns*** *(Pronomen)* ***I, you, he, she, it, we, you, they*** gebildet. Dies ist aber auch bei ***nouns*** *(Nomen)* möglich, jedoch nur in der 3. Person Singular.

*My mother **has got** a new job.*	*My mother**'s got** a new job.*
*Anna **has got** two brothers.*	*Anna**'s got** two brothers.*

3 Short forms of *has got* and *to be*

☛ In der 3. Person Singular darf die Kurzform von ***has got*** nicht mit der Kurzform von ***to be*** verwechselt werden. Das ***got*** zeigt dir an, dass es sich um die Kurzform von ***has got*** handelt.

short forms	long forms
*David**'s got** a new bike.*	*David **has got** a new bike.*
*David**'s** a nice boy.*	*David **is** a nice boy.*

☛ Die Form ***to have*** (ohne ***got***) kann die Bedeutung *etwas zu sich nehmen, essen* haben. Nur in diesem Fall kann man das Verb auch ins ***present progressive*** *(die Verlaufsform des Präsens)* setzen.

*I usually **have** muesli for breakfast.*	Ich **esse** normalerweise Müsli zum Frühstück.
*She**'s having** dinner now.*	Sie **isst** gerade zu Abend.

EXERCISE 1 Long forms and short forms. Write these sentences again and use the short forms of **have got / has got** if you can. Be careful: sometimes you can't use a short form.

Tom and Jack are brothers. They have got a sister, too.

Tom and Jack are brothers. They've got a sister, too.

Tom has got a big room on the first floor.

____.

He has got a bed, a cupboard and a sofa in his room.

____.

Jack and his sister Sue have got two rooms in the attic.

____.

They have got cupboards and beds, too, of course.

____.

And their dog? It has got a big basket in Jack's room.

____.

EXERCISE 2 Put in **have got** or **has got.** Use the long forms here.

Jack ________________ a lot of books in his room. He likes books and he reads a lot. Some of his books ________________ more than 500 pages. He ________________ stories about monsters and vampires. His sister Sue thinks that these books are silly. She ________________ some books about history and geography. The two children ________________ very different ideas about books.

EXERCISE 3 Put in the short forms of **have got / has got: 've got / 's got.**

Jack: "Hey Sue. Look, I __________ a new vampire story!"

Sue: "Oh no, not again. We__________ so many books, Jack. And your stories are terrible."

Jack: "It__________ about 400 pages. I can read it in three days, Sue."

Sue: "Wow, you__________ too much free time then. Oh listen, Mum and Dad are calling. Dad__________ lots of shopping bags in the car. We must help him."

EXERCISE 4 What have Jack and Sue got? Look at the pictures and write down the sentences.

Jack has got a dog.

EXERCISE 5 What have you, your family and your friends got? Write down sentences. You can use the long or the short forms.

I / My best friend / My sister / My brother / My parents	have got / has got 've got / 's got	a cat / a CD / a house / a flat / a school bag / a stereo / a book / a pet / a bike / a nice smile / good ideas

I have got a school bag.

Exercise 1

Tom and Jack are brothers. They have got a sister, too.
Tom and Jack are brothers. They**'ve** got a sister, too.

Tom has got a big room on the first floor.
Tom**'s got** a big room on the first floor.

He has got a bed, a cupboard and a sofa in his room.
He**'s got** a bed, a cupboard and a sofa in his room.

Jack and his sister Sue have got two rooms in the attic.
Jack and his sister Sue **have got** two rooms in the attic.

Hier keine Kurzform möglich! Dies ginge nur bei einem Namen in der 3. Person Singular, z. B.: Sue**'s got** a room in the attic.

They have got cupboards and beds, too, of course.
They**'ve got** cupboards and beds, too, of course.

And their dog? It has got a big basket in Jack's room.
And their dog? It**'s got** a big basket in Jack's room.

Exercise 2

Jack **has got** a lot of books in his room. He likes books and he reads a lot. Some of his books **have got** more than 500 pages. He **has got** stories about monsters and vampires. His sister Sue thinks that these books are silly. She **has got** some books about history and geography. The two children **have got** very different ideas about books.

Exercise 3

Jack: "Hey Sue. Look, I**'ve got** a new vampire story!"
Sue: "Oh no, not again. We**'ve got** so many books, Jack. And your stories are terrible."
Jack: "It**'s got** about 400 pages. I can read it in three days, Sue."
Sue: "Wow, you**'ve got** too much free time then. Oh listen, Mum and Dad are calling. Dad**'s got** lots of shopping bags in the car. We must help him."

Exercise 4

Jack **has got** a dog.
Jack **has got** a computer.
Jack **has got** two books.
Sue and Jack **have got** a ball.
Sue and Jack **have got** a skateboard.
Sue **has got** two CDs.
Sue **has got** a rucksack.

Exercise 5

Hier sind individuelle Lösungen möglich.

Lösungsbeispiele:
I **have got** a stereo. / I**'ve got** a stereo (Die Kurzform ist hier möglich, da **I** ein Pronomen ist.)
My best friend **has got** a book. / My best friend**'s got** a book. (Die Kurzform ist hier möglich, da es sich um ein Nomen in der 3. Person Singular handelt.)
My sister **has got** a nice smile. / My sister**'s got** a nice smile.
My brother **has got** good ideas. / My brother**'s got** good ideas.
My parents **have got** a flat. (Hier ist keine Kurzform möglich.)

Achte beim Korrigieren auf die Unterscheidung zwischen **have got** und **has got:**
I / My parents **have got** ... My best friend / My sister / My brother **has got** ...

ANSWER KEY ANSWER KEY ANSWER KEY

14 *Have got:* negatives, questions, short answers (Verneinungen, Fragen, Kurzantworten mit *have got*)

1 The negation of *have got*

Sätze mit ***have got/has got*** werden verneint, indem man ***not*** zwischen ***have/has*** und ***got*** einfügt. In der gesprochenen Sprache wird ***not*** in der Regel zu ***n't*** verkürzt und an ***have/has*** angehängt.

positive sentence	negative sentence (long form)	negative sentence (short form)
I have got a garden.	*I have **not** got a garden.*	*I have**n't** got a garden.*
You have got a pet.	*You have **not** got a pet.*	*You have**n't** got a pet.*
He/She/It has got lots of toys.	*He/She/It has **not** got lots of toys.*	*He/She/It has**n't** got lots of toys.*
We have got a nice teacher.	*We have **not** got a nice teacher.*	*We have**n't** got a nice teacher.*
You have got a day off.	*You have **not** got a day off.*	*You have**n't** got a day off.*
They have got new pencils.	*They have **not** got new pencils.*	*They have**n't** got new pencils.*

2 Questions with *have got*

Bei der Fragebildung wird ***have/has*** vor das Subjekt (hier: ***you, she***) gestellt, ***got*** bleibt hinter dem Subjekt.

Vergleiche Aussagesatz	***You have got** a nice pet.*	***She has got** lots of time now.*
und Fragesatz	***Have you got** a nice pet?*	***Has she got** lots of time now?*

3 Short answers with *have got/has got*

Bei den ***short answers*** *(Kurzantworten)* wird ***have/has*** aus der Frage noch einmal aufgegriffen, das ***got*** lässt man weg.

In den ***short answers*** mit ***yes*** sind *keine* ***short forms*** möglich. Man spricht und schreibt also immer die ***long form,*** z. B. ***Yes, I have.***

questions	short answers with yes	short answers with no
Have you got a CD?	***Yes, I have.***	***No, I haven't.***
Have I got enough time?	***Yes, you have.***	***No, you haven't.***
Has he/she/it got a toy?	***Yes, he/she/it has.***	***No, he/she/it hasn't.***
Have we got a new teacher?	***Yes, we have.***	***No, we haven't.***
Have you got a small classroom?	***Yes, you have.***	***No, you haven't.***
Have they got posters on their walls?	***Yes, they have.***	***No, they haven't.***

In der Regel klingt eine ***short answer*** viel höflicher als nur ***Yes/No*** allein.

EXERCISE 1 Daniel, Leo and their rooms. Write down correct sentences and questions.

1 Daniel / got / football posters / in his room / has

____?

2 the two boys / have / in their rooms / sofas / got

____?

3 skates / and a skateboard / has / Daniel / got / in his room

____.

4 hasn't / any football posters / got / he

____.

5 his room / is / Leo / a sofa / got / hasn't / because / too small

____.

EXERCISE 2 In the classroom. What have the children, Mrs Brown and you got? Ask questions and give short answers.

	Joe	all the girls	Daniel and Leo	Mrs Brown	you
a pencil case?	yes	yes	no	no	?
ten pounds?	no	no	yes	yes	?

Has Joe got a pencil case? – Yes, he has.

Have all the girls got pencil cases? – Yes, ________.

____.

____.

____.

____.

____.

____.

____.

____.

____.

____.

Exercise 3 Daniel and Leo's shopping list. Look at the list and fill in the missing words: negations, questions and short answers with **have got / has got.**

Mum: "Hi Daniel. Are you back from the supermarket?
__________________________ everything?"

Daniel: "No, _____________________ .
Sorry. I _____________ pencils and a ruler.
But I _______________________ the new pens.
Oh Mum, school things aren't easy to find in the supermarket."

Mum: "What are you saying? You ________________________ the pens?
And your brother Leo? __________________________ two exercise books and a folder?"

Daniel: "No, ________________________. But we can buy the things tomorrow."

Mum: "Tomorrow?? No, I will call Mrs Kimberly now and ask her."

Exercise 4 Daniel's and Leo's mum is calling Mrs Kimberly. Her daughter Charlotte is in one class with the two boys. Listen to what the two women are saying and choose the correct answers.

1 Leo and Daniel ...
■ have got lots of folders at home.
■ have got some green folders at home.
■ haven't got any red folders.

2 Leo and Daniel ...
■ haven't got rulers or pencils.
■ have got a ruler, a rubber and pencils.
■ are not sure if they have got a pencil.

3 Leo and Daniel's mum thinks that ...
■ they haven't got folders
■ there are no pens at home
■ they have got lots of pens

4 Mrs Kimberly ...
■ wants to buy a new ruler for her daughter Charlotte.
■ knows that Charlotte hasn't got a pen.
■ asks her friend to go to the cinema with her.

Exercise 1
1 **Has** Daniel **got** football posters in his room?
2 **Have** the two boys **got** sofas in their rooms?
3 Daniel **has got** skates and a skateboard in his room.
4 He **hasn't got** any football posters.
5 Leo **hasn't got** a sofa because his room is too small.

Exercise 2
Has Joe **got** a pencil case? - **Yes, he has.**
Have all the girls **got** pencil cases? - **Yes, they have.**
Have Daniel and Leo **got** pencil cases? - **No, they haven't.**
Has Mrs Brown **got** a pencil case? - **No, she hasn't.**
Have you **got** a pencil case? - **Yes, I have / No, I haven't.**
Has Joe **got** ten pounds? - **No, he hasn't.**
Have all the girls **got** ten pounds? - **No, they haven't.**
Have Daniel and Leo **got** ten pounds? - **Yes, they have.**
Has Mrs Brown **got** ten pounds? - **Yes, she has.**
Have you **got** ten pounds? - **Yes, I have / No, I haven't.**

Exercise 3
Mum: "Hi Daniel. Are you back from the supermarket? **Have you got** everything?"
Daniel: "No, **we haven't** / No, **I haven't.** Sorry. I **have got** / **I've got** pencils and a ruler.
But I **haven't got** the new pens. Oh Mum, school things aren't easy to find in the supermarket."
Mum: "What are you saying? You **have not got / haven't got** the pens? And your brother Leo? **Has he got** two exercise books and a folder?"
Daniel: "No, **he hasn't.** But we can buy the things tomorrow."
Mum: "Tomorrow?? No, I will call Mrs Kimberly now and ask her."

Exercise 4
1 Leo and Daniel ...
- **have got lots of folders at home.**
- have got some green folders at home.
- haven't got any red folders.

2 Leo and Daniel ...
- haven't got rulers or pencils.
- **have got a ruler, a rubber and pencils.**
- are not sure if they have got a pencil.

3 Leo and Daniel's mum thinks that ...
- they haven't got folders.
- **there are no pens at home.**
- they have got lots of pens.

4 Mrs Kimberly ...
- wants to buy a new ruler for her daughter Charlotte.
- **knows that Charlotte hasn't got a pen.**
- asks her friend to go to the cinema with her.

Geh bei Hörverstehensaufgaben immer folgendermaßen vor:
Lies dir zuerst die Aufgaben genau durch, damit du weißt, worauf du hören sollst. Die Aufgaben geben dir schon einen Überblick, worum es in dem Text gehen wird. Kläre unbekannte Wörter mit Hilfe des Wörterbuchs, falls nötig.
Beim ersten Anhören sollst du versuchen, den Text als Ganzes zu erfassen, also zu verstehen, worum es im Großen und Ganzen geht. Einige der leichteren Ankreuzaufgaben wirst du dabei schon lösen können.
Beim zweiten Anhören musst du dann verstärkt versuchen, dich auf Einzelheiten zu konzentrieren, nach denen gefragt wird.
Nur wenn dir der Text große Probleme bereitet, hörst du ihn dir noch ein drittes Mal an.

Listing comprehension

Exercise 1 Read the sentences. Then listen to the text and find the right answers.

1	Terfel is from ...	England	Wales	Winnipeg
2	Swansea is a city in England.	true		false
3	Terfel is a ... dragon.	red	yellow	green
4	Steve is new in London.	true		false
5	The children are in class 5ST.	true		false
6	The English teacher is a man.	true		false
7	The English teacher is ...	Mr Taken	nice	from Wales
8	The park is ______________________ Cecily's house.			
9	Steve is a good football player.	true		false
10	______________________ is the best football player.			
11	The football is ...	white & yellow	yellow & blue	blue & white
12	______________________ has got a good idea.			
13	A ... can help the children.	mouse	dog	cat
14/15	The football is in a ______________, but then it is	in /	on /	under
	the grass again.			

15 P

Verbs

It is the next day. Cecily, Steve and Terfel are at school again. Today they have got English, then they have got German with Mr Beemer and Music with Mr Note.

They're in their Music class now.

Exercise 2 Put in the right forms of the verbs.

Mr Note: "Good morning, boys and girls! Please ______________ (sit) down!"

Class: "Good morning, sir!"

Mr Note: "______________________ (have got / you) your homework?"

Cecily: "No, I ______________(not to have). Sorry!"

Mr Note: "That ________________ (not to be) good. Please ________________ (not to forget) your homework again. OK, let's start. We ______________________ (have got) a nice class today. Steve ______________________ (have got) his guitar with him."

Steve: "Yes, I ________________. It ________________ (to be) over there."

Mr Note: "Then ______________________ (to fetch) it, please. But __ ______________________ (not to start) to play. The class ______________________ (not have got) the song. But here it ________________ (to be)."

Now the pupils ______________________ (have got) the song in their hands, and they can all sing together.

14P

It is the afternoon now. Terfel Dragon and his parents are shopping because Terfel needs a new school uniform.

Plural forms, genitive forms, short forms, short answers

EXERCISE 3A **s, 's or s'?** Put in the right **plural** or **genitive form of nouns** or **short form of verbs.**

The Dragon___ aren't happy with Terfel___ school uniform. So now they are at a shop to get a new uniform. It___ a nice uniform. It___ got grey trousers and a white shirt. There is a pullover, too. It___ blue. When Terfel and his parents go outside again, they can see Cecily___ family___ bike shop. Cecily___ father is there, and the Dragon___ house is nearby.

8P

EXERCISE 3B Look at the text again. What do these **short forms** stand for?

1 It's a nice uniform. → ______________________

2 It's got grey trousers. → ______________________

3 It's blue. → ______________________

3P

EXERCISE 4 Later in the afternoon. Look at the picture and say if the statements are true or false. Use **short answers.** If the answer is no, correct the statement.

1 There are two clouds in the sky. 1 P

____

2 There is a tree in front of the house. 3 P

____

3 Terfel has got a banana in his hands. 3 P

____

4 He is on a box. 1 P

____

5 The three mice are under the box. 3 P

____

6 Cecily is in a tree. 3 P

____

7 Steve and Terfel have got T-shirts on. 3 P

____

8 There are five flowers in the picture. 1 P

____

Exercise 5 Petra from Germany is in the park, too. But she can't speak English. Can you help the children?

Petra: „Hallo, ihr drei. Ich bin Petra. Seid ihr aus London?"

You: "____

____?"

6 P

Steve: "Yes, we are. I'm Steve and this is Terfel and Cecily. Where are you from?"

You: „____

____?"

4 P

Cecily: "And have you got our football? I can't find it."

You: „____

____."

3 P

Petra: „Ich komme aus Coburg in Deutschland. Aber ich habe euren Fußball nicht."

You: "____

____."

5 P

Together they find their football and then they play with Petra.

Exercise 6 Later at Steve's home. Put in the right **prepositions.**

Steve's mum: "It's nice that you're home now. Please wash your hands. Dinner is __________ ten minutes."

Steve: "OK, Mum. Can I put my inline skates in the garage __________ I wash my hands? I can go __________ the bathroom after that."

Steve's mum: "Yes, of course. And then you can go to your father's hobby room. Tell him dinner is __________ seven."

Steve: "OK. So I have to wash my hands and talk to Dad __________ dinner and I can watch TV __________ dinner."

Steve's mum: "That's fine. And can you please put those glasses over there __________ the cupboard and the flowers __________ the table?"

8 P

Reading comprehension: Steve's family

EXERCISE 7 Read the text and find useful information to answer the questions below.

Steve is a boy from a nice family. He hasn't got a sister or a brother, but he has got a cat and a dog. Steve's family name is Green. His mother's name is Sue and his father's name is Alan. The Green family's house is in Kendal Road. It's a nice house with blue windows, a black roof and two garages. One garage is for their grey car, and the other garage is where they put a lot of things: Steve's bike, the family's inline skates and all the things they don't want in the house. The house has got a big garden, too. Buster the dog and Jazzy the cat like to play there.

Steve's dad Alan has got a nice hobby: he invents things! He has got ideas for new things and then he makes them. Alan is a drummer, too. Sue Green's hobby is playing the piano. So with Steve's guitar, the family has got three instruments – they are a little band! When they have got time, they make music together.

1	How many people are in Steve's family?	two	three	four
2	There are two cats in the family.	true		false
3	What's the dog's name?	It's ______.		
4	Are the windows of the house green?	______, they ______.		
5	The family has got two cars.	true	false	
6	Mrs Green can play the piano.	true	false	
7	What instruments has the family got?	______		
8	Alan Green invents things. Look at the text again and find out what that is in *German:*	Alan Green ______.		

10 P

EXERCISE 8 Plurals. Here are some words from the text. Put them in the plural.

singular	plural
boy	______
family	______
this	______
piano	______
house	______
man	______

6 P

Auswertung Trage rechts deine Gesamtpunktzahl ein und vergleiche.

☺ 100 – 76 points	😐 75 – 51 points	☹ 50 – 0 points

TOTAL SCORE 100 P

Exercise 1

1	Terfel is from …	England	✗ **Wales**	Winnipeg
2	Swansea is a city in England.	true		✗ **false**
3	Terfel is a … dragon.	✗ **red**	yellow	green
4	Steve is new in London.	true		✗ **false**
5	The children are in class 5ST.	✗ **true**		false
6	The English teacher is a man.	true		✗ **false**
7	The English teacher is …	Mr Taken	✗ **nice**	from Wales
8	The park is **behind** Cecily's house.			
9	Steve is a good football player.	✗ **true**		false
10	**Cecily** is the best football player.			
11	The football is …	✗ **white & yellow**	yellow & blue	blue & white
12	**Terfel** has got a good idea.			
13	A … can help the children.	mouse	dog	✗ **cat**
14/15	The football is in a **tree,** but then it is in / ✗ **on** / under the grass again.			

Exercise 2

sit | Have you got | haven't | isn't | don't forget | have got ('ve got) | has got ('s got) | have | is ('s) | fetch | don't start | hasn't got | is | have got

Exercise 3A

The Dragon**s** aren't happy with Terfel**'s** school uniform. So now they are at a shop to get a new uniform. It**'s** a nice uniform. It**'s** got grey trousers and a white shirt. There is a pullover, too. It**'s** blue. When Terfel and his parents go outside again, they can see Cecily**'s** family**'s** bike shop. Cecily**'s** father is there, and the Dragon**s'** house is nearby.

Exercise 3B

1 It's a nice uniform. → **it is** 2 It's got grey trousers. → **it has**
3 It's blue. → **it is**

Exercise 4

1 Yes, there are. 2 No, there isn't. There's a bush in front of the house. 3 No, he hasn't. He has got (He's got) a ball in his hands. 4 Yes, he is. 5 No, they aren't. They're in the box. 6 No, she isn't. She's behind a tree. 7 No, they haven't. Steve's got a pullover and Terfel's got nothing on. 8 Yes, there are.

Exercise 5

"Hello, you three. I'm Petra. Are you from London?"
„Ja. Ich bin Steve und das da sind Terfel und Cecily. Woher kommst du?"
„Und hast du unseren Fußball? Ich kann ihn nicht finden."
"I'm from Coburg in Germany. But I haven't got your football."

Exercise 6

in | before | to | at | before – after | into – onto

Exercise 7

1	How many people are in Steve's family?	two ✗ **three** four
2	There are two cats in the family.	true ✗ **false**
3	What's the dog's name?	It's **Buster.**
4	Are the windows of the house green?	**No,** they **aren't.**
5	The family has got two cars.	true ✗ **false**
6	Mrs Green can play the piano.	✗ **true** false
7	What instruments has the family got?	**drums, guitar, piano**
8	Alan Green **erfindet Sachen / Er ist ein Erfinder.**	

Exercise 8

Plural forms: boy**s**, famil**ies**, **these,** piano**s,** hous**es,** m**e**n

ANSWER KEY ANSWER KEY ANSWER KEY

15 *Can* and *must* in statements and *yes/no* questions (*Can* und *must* in Aussagen und Entscheidungsfragen)

Can und ***must*** sind modale Hilfsverben. Die Form der modalen Hilfsverben ist für alle Personen gleich, d. h. in der 3. Person Singular wird im Unterschied zu anderen Verben kein ***-s*** angehängt. Dem modalen Hilfsverb folgt im Aussagesatz ein Verb im Infinitiv, der Grundform des Verbs, ohne ***to.***
Fragen mit ***must*** und ***can*** werden ohne ***do*** gebildet. Sie beginnen jeweils mit dem Hilfsverb.

1 *Must* and *can* in statements

Can *(können / dürfen)* drückt aus, dass man etwas tun kann oder darf. ***Must*** *(müssen)* hingegen beschreibt im Aussagesatz eine Verpflichtung oder eine Notwendigkeit, d. h. dass jemand etwas tun muss, oder es notwendig ist, dass etwas geschieht.

I	**can**	*come*	*to your party.*	Ich **kann / darf** zu deiner Party kommen.
You	**must**	*invite*	*Jenny too.*	Du **musst** Jenny auch einladen.
She	**can**	*tell*	*funny jokes.*	Sie **kann** lustige Witze erzählen.
We	**must**	*bring*	*presents.*	Wir **müssen** Geschenke mitbringen.
You	**can**	*play*	*lots of games.*	Ihr **könnt** viele Spiele spielen.
They	**must**	*be*	*there at 3 pm.*	Sie **müssen** um 15 Uhr da sein.

Must kann auch in Annahmen verwendet werden:
That ***must*** *be our new neighbour.* – Das **muss wohl** unser neuer Nachbar sein.

2 *Must* and *can* in *yes/no* questions

Yes/no questions sind Fragen, die man mit Ja oder Nein beantworten muss *(Entscheidungsfragen).* Beachte die Satzstellung: ***Must*** und ***can*** stehen am Anfang der Entscheidungsfrage, danach folgt das Subjekt und dann das Verb.

Can	*I*	*go*	*to Austin's party?*	*Yes, you can.*
Must	*we*	*bring*	*presents?*	*Yes, you must.*
Can	*they*	*play*	*games?*	*Yes, they can.*

Entscheidungsfragen können mit einer Kurzantwort beantwortet werden. Nach ***yes*** oder ***no*** werden dazu das Pronomen und das Hilfsverb noch einmal aufgenommen:

- *Yes, you* ***can.***
- *No, you* ***can't.***

EXERCISE 1 Tick the correct sentence.

Sandra must find a present for Austin at the shop. ____
Sandra must to find a present for Austin at the shop. ____

Austin can to invite ten friends to his party. ____
Austin can invite ten friends to his party. ____

Must they bring a sleeping bag? ____
Bring they must a sleeping bag? ____

Can I drink juice with dinner? ____
Can I to drink juice with dinner? ____

EXERCISE 2 Say what you **can / must** do in these places.

What **can** you do here?

1 In the library: ________________________________

2 In the park: ________________________________

3 At the seaside: ________________________________

What **must** we do here?

4 In Mr Brown's classroom: ________________________________

5 On the bus: ________________________________

6 At grandma's farm: ________________________________

EXERCISE 3 Give short answers.

Can you speak English? Yes, ________________.

Must they do their homework? Yes, ________________.

Can I have ice cream after dinner? Yes, ________________.

Must he go home now? Yes, ________________.

Can we eat sandwiches? Yes, ________________.

Must she take the bus? Yes, ________________.

Exercise 4 Mum's to-do list. Today Austin's mum is not at home. Here is a to-do list for Austin, his sister Sandra and their dad. What **must** they do? What **can** they do at night?

Austin ______________________ and he ______________________

______________________. Sandra ______________________

______________________. They ______________________

______________________. At night, they ______________________

______________________ or they ______________________.

Exercise 5 Form correct sentences with the words below.

1 invitations / Austin / must / for his birthday / send

______________________.

2 come / Jacob and Sandra / can / to the party

______________________.

3 must / a cake / bring / they

______________________.

4 the night / at Austin's house / can / stay / you

______________________?

5 we / can / a movie / after the party / watch

______________________?

Exercise 1

Sandra must find a present for Austin at the shop.	✓
Sandra must to find a present for Austin at the shop.	–
Austin can to invite ten friends to his party.	–
Austin can invite ten friends to his party.	✓
Must they bring a sleeping bag?	✓
Bring they must a sleeping bag?	–
Can I drink juice with dinner?	✓
Can I to drink juice with dinner?	–

Exercise 2

What **can** you do here?

1 In the library: I **can read** (books / a book).
2 In the park: I **can play** (soccer).
3 At the seaside: I **can swim** (in the sea).

What **must** we do here?

4 In Mr Brown's classroom: We **must sing** (songs).
5 On the bus: We **must sit down.**
6 At grandma's farm: We **must milk** the cows.

Exercise 3

Can you speak English?	Yes, **I can.**
Must they do their homework?	Yes, **they must.**
Can I have ice cream after dinner?	Yes, **you can.**
Must he go home now?	Yes, **he must.**
Can we eat sandwiches?	Yes, **we can.**
Must she take the bus?	Yes, **she must.**

Exercise 4

Austin must eat lunch and he must do his homework.
Sandra must take the dog for a walk.
They must wash the car and prepare dinner.
At night, they can watch TV or they can read.

Exercise 5

1 invitations / Austin / must / for his birthday / send
Austin must send invitations for his birthday.

2 come / Jacob and Sandra / can / to the party
Jacob and Sandra can come to the party.

3 must / a cake / bring / they
They must bring a cake.

4 the night / at Austin's house / can / stay / you
Can you stay the night at Austin's house?

5 we / can / a movie / after the party / watch
Can we watch a movie after the party?

16 *Have to/must:* necessity or obligation (Notwendigkeit oder Pflicht ausdrücken mit *have to/must*)

1 *Must* in statements

Um auszudrücken, dass man selbst oder jemand anderes etwas tun muss, verwendet man das modale Hilfsverb ***must.*** Es gibt nur diese eine Form, d. h. ***must*** wird in allen Personen gleich konjugiert (genau wie ***can***). ***Must*** steht immer vor dem Infinitiv des Vollverbs (aber ohne ***to***). In englischen Aussagesätzen steht das Vollverb immer hinter ***must,*** im Deutschen steht es dagegen am Ende des Satzes.

*I **must feed** my dog.*	Ich **muss** meinen Hund **füttern.**
*Jill **must get** up early to catch the bus.*	Jill **muss** früh aufstehen, um den Bus **zu kriegen.**

Es gibt keine ***short form*** *(Kurzform)* von ***must. Must*** wird nur im Präsens verwendet.

2 *Have to* in statements

Die Ersatzform von ***must*** ist ***have to,*** und dies zwangsweise in allen anderen Zeitformen außer dem ***simple present. Have to*** wird genau wie das Verb ***to have*** konjugiert, d. h. nur in der 3. Person Singular im Präsens ändert sich die Form zu ***has to.***

*I **have to** work at the weekend.*	Ich **muss** am Wochenende arbeiten.
*This homework **has to** be handed in on Wednesday.*	Diese Hausaufgabe **muss** am Mittwoch abgegeben werden.
*We **had to** do the shopping for our parents.*	Wir **mussten** für unsere Eltern einkaufen.

Es gibt keine ***short form*** von ***have to/has to.***

Must drückt aus, was man selbst unbedingt tun möchte, was man entschieden hat oder woran man fest glaubt, wohingegen ***have to*** Zwang oder Notwendigkeit durch eine andere Person/Institution oder durch äußere Umstände vermittelt.

*I **must** buy this book (because I want to read it).*	Ich **muss unbedingt** dieses Buch kaufen (weil ich es lesen möchte).
*I **have to** buy this book (because I need it at school).*	Ich **muss** dieses Buch kaufen (weil ich es in der Schule brauche).

3 *Have to* in questions

Fragen werden im Allgemeinen mit ***have to*** formuliert. Um eine Frage mit ***have to*** zu bilden, benutzt man ***do/does*** wie mit anderen Vollverben (→ Modul 30).

***Do** I **have to** do work at the weekend? Yes, you **do**.*	**Muss** ich am Wochenende arbeiten? Ja, du **musst.**
***Does** this homework **have to** be handed in on Wednesday? Yes, it **does**.*	**Muss** diese Hausaufgabe am Mittwoch abgegeben werden? Ja, sie **muss.**
***Did** you **have to** do the shopping for your parents? Yes, we **did**.*	**Musstet** ihr für eure Eltern einkaufen? Ja, wir **mussten.** (= keine Form von ***must*** möglich!)

Exercise 1 What do they **have to** do? Write sentences.

	take out the rubbish	buy milk	dust, clean room	water plants	mow lawn
Tom		X	X		X
Lea			X	X	
Mike	X		X		
Minni	X		X		

1 ______________________________.

2 ______________________________.

3 ______________________________.

4 ______________________________.

5 ______________________________.

Exercise 2 Poor Tom! Fill in the correct form: **have to** or **has to.**

Tom ____________ get up every day at 7 o'clock. He ____________ wash and then he ____________ get dressed. His mother calls: "Tom, you ____________ hurry, you are late again!" So Tom ____________ run to catch the bus; on the bus he ____________ breathe *(= atmen)* deeply because he is so out of breath. He meets his friends there, but they ____________ be quiet and not disturb *(= stören)* other people. The bus arrives at school late, so he and his friends ____________ hurry up. The pupils ____________ be in their classroom at 8 o'clock. Everybody ____________ to stand up when the teacher enters the room. The children ____________ greet their teacher, and then they ____________ sit down. As the weather outside is fine, it is hard for Tom, but he ____________ concentrate to get good marks. But Tom starts thinking about what he ____________ do when he gets home: "I ____________ clean my guinea pig's cage and I ____________ do the washing-up. Then I must do my homework quickly because I want to go swimming." The teacher calls Tom: "Tom, you are dreaming again! You ____________ pay attention!" Tom is happy when school is finally over, but when he comes home, his father says: "Tom, first you ____________ help me in the garden!" ...

EXERCISE 3 Write questions with **to have to.** Give short answers.

1 Muss sie den Hasen füttern? Ja, sie muss.

____.

2 Musst du das Fahrrad reparieren? Ja, ich muss.

____.

3 Muss George den Hund ausführen? Ja, er muss.

____.

4 Müssen wir das Fußballspiel gewinnen? Ja, wir müssen.

____.

EXERCISE 4 Write sentences with these words.

1 window / I / open / the / teacher / the / because / me / asked / have to / to / do it ____.

2 Caroline / blackboard / have to / Does / the / clean

____?

3 You / this / see / movie / science fiction / must

____!

4 pay / driving / they / money / have to / for / fast / too / Do

____?

5 has to / homework / says / he / this afternoon / finish / He / his

____.

6 my / come to / must / party / You / birthday

____!

EXERCISE 5 Choose the right verb: **must** or **to have to?**

1 I like Korean! I ___________ speak Korean well.

2 I need Chinese for my job. I ___________ speak Chinese well.

3 One of our school rules reads: "Wear the school uniform." I ___________ wear it.

4 I want to look good. I ___________ buy a new suit.

Exercise 1

	take out the rubbish	buy milk	dust, clean room	water plants	mow Lawn
Tom		X	X		X
Lea			X	X	
Mike	X		X		
Minni	X		X		

1 Mike and Minni **have to** take out the rubbish.
2 Tom **has to** buy milk.
3 Tom, Lea and Mike and Minni (or: All of them) **have to** dust and clean their rooms.
4 Lea **has to** water the plants.
5 Tom **has to** mow the lawn.

Exercise 2

Tom **has to** get up every day at 7 o'clock. He **has to** wash and then he **has to** get dressed. His mother calls: "Tom, you **have to** hurry, you are late again!"
So Tom **has to** run to catch the bus; on the bus he **has to** breathe (= atmen) deeply because he is so out of breath. He meets his friends there, but they **have to** be quiet and not disturb (= stören) the other people. The bus arrives at school late, so he and his friends **have to** hurry up. The pupils **have to** be in their classroom at 8 o'clock. Everybody **has to** stand up when the teacher enters the room. The children **have to** greet their teacher, and then they **have to** sit down. As the weather outside is fine, it is hard for Tom, but he **has to** concentrate to get good marks. But Tom starts thinking about what he **has to** do when he gets home: "I **have to** clean my guinea pig's cage and I **have to** do the washing-up. Then I must do my homework quickly because I want to go swimming." The teacher calls Tom: "Tom, you are dreaming again! You **have to** pay attention!" Tom is happy when school is finally over, but when he comes home, his father says: "Tom, first you **have to** help me in the garden!"

Exercise 3

1 Muss sie den Hasen füttern? Ja, sie muss.
Does she **have to** feed the rabbit? Yes, she **does.**
2 Musst du das Fahrrad reparieren? Ja, ich muss.
Do you **have to** repair the bicycle? Yes, I **do.**
3 Muss George den Hund ausführen? Ja, er muss.
Does George **have to** walk the dog? Yes, he **does.**
4 Müssen wir das Fußballspiel gewinnen? Ja, wir müssen.
Do we **have to** win the football match? Yes, we **do.**

Exercise 4

1 **I have to open the window because the teacher asked me to do it.**
2 **Does Caroline have to clean the blackboard?**
3 **You must see this science fiction movie!**
4 **Do they have to pay money for driving too fast?**
5 **He says he has to finish his homework this afternoon.**
6 **You must come to my birthday party!**

Exercise 5

1 I like Korean! I **must** speak Korean well.
2 I need Chinese for my job. I **have to** speak Chinese well.
3 One of our school rules reads: "Wear the school uniform."
I **have to** wear it.
4 I want to look good. I **must** buy a new suit.

ANSWER KEY ANSWER KEY ANSWER KEY

17 *Can/can't/may* in statements and questions (*Can/can't/may* in Aussagesätzen und Fragen)

1 *Can* and *can't* in statements

Das modale Hilfsverb ***can*** *(können/dürfen)* und seine verneinte Form ***can't*** stehen immer mit dem Infinitiv, der Grundform des Vollverbs, **ohne *to.*** Anstatt ***can't*** wird im Schriftlichen manchmal auch ***cannot*** verwendet.

Can und ***can't*** (bzw. ***cannot***) bleiben in allen Personen gleich. Es gibt hier also kein angehängtes ***-s*** bei ***he, she, it*** in der 3. Person Singular.

I ***can play*** *football in the garden.*	Ich **kann** Fußball im Garten **spielen.**
He ***can speak*** *English.*	Er **kann** Englisch **sprechen.**
You ***can't go*** *to the party.*	Du **kannst nicht** zur Fete **gehen.**
They ***cannot listen*** *to the CD.*	Sie **können** die CD **nicht anhören.**

In englischen Aussagesätzen steht das Vollverb immer hinter ***can*** bzw. ***can't,*** im Deutschen steht das Vollverb jedoch am Ende, wie du in den Beispielen sehen kannst.

2 *Can* and *can't* in questions

Um eine Frage zu bilden, stellt man ***can*** wie im Deutschen einfach an den Satzanfang. Die gleiche Regel gilt für die verneinte Form ***can't*** (oder ***cannot***).

Oft wird ***can*** benutzt, um höflich um etwas zu bitten, um Erlaubnis zu fragen oder um auszudrücken, ob jemand etwas tun darf oder auch nicht.

We	***can*** *watch TV.*	Wir	**dürfen** fernsehen.
Can	*we watch TV?*	**Dürfen**	wir fernsehen?
Can't	*we watch TV?*	**Können**	wir **nicht** fernsehen?
Can	*we* ***not*** *watch TV?*		

Man kann ***can***-Fragen auch mit einem vorangestellten zusätzlichen Fragewort bilden:

Where ***can*** *they go?*	Wohin **können** sie gehen?
Why ***can't*** *she do that?*	Wieso **kann** sie das nicht **tun?**

3 *Can* in short answers

Auch in Kurzantworten gibt es nur die eine Form von ***can*** und ***can't*** (bzw. ***cannot***).

Can *we watch TV?*	*Yes, you* ***can.***
Can't *you show me the way?*	*No, sorry, I* ***can't.*** */ No, sorry, I* ***cannot.***

Wenn man besonders höflich fragen will, benutzt man ***may*** statt ***can.***

May *I open the door for you?*	**Darf** ich Ihnen die Tür öffnen?
Yes, you ***may.*** *Thank you.*	Ja, danke, du **darfst.**

Exercise 1 Which answer is correct: **can** or **can't?** Look at the pictures and underline the correct answer.

Can the man jump?	Can the woman hear?	Can the biker fly?

a) Yes, he can. b) No, he can't.	a) No, she can't. b) Yes, she can.	a) Yes, he can. b) No, he can't.
Can the man swim?	**Can the cat play?**	**Can he run?**

a) No, he can't. b) Yes, he can.	a) Yes, it can. b) No, it can't.	a) Yes, he can. b) No, he can't.

Exercise 2 Fill in **can** or **can't,** according to the situation.

1 Marc and Tim are good at the saxophone; they ______ play the saxophone well.

2 You know the answer to the question! You ______ answer the question.

3 Marianne can speak English, but she ______ speak Korean.

4 I am very nervous today! I ______ sleep.

5 Joseph ______ play basketball very well: he is an excellent basketball player.

6 This test is very difficult; I ______ answer any of the questions.

Exercise 3 Look at the sentences and form questions with **können** and **can.**

Wir **dürfen** hier drinnen spielen. ______________________________?	We ***can*** play in here. ______________________________?
Sie **kann** dein Telefon benutzen. ______________________________?	She **can** use your telephone. ______________________________?

Exercise 4 Write sentences or questions with these words.

1 go / We / swimming / tomorrow / can

____.

2 John / speak / Can't / English

____?

3 sugar / Can / the / I / please / have

____?

4 school / to / You / today / go / can't / ill / are / because / you

____.

5 TV / She / because / broken / it's / can't / watch

____.

6 cook / for / Saturday / they / on / lunch / can / What

____?

7 get / we / taxi / a / can / Where

____?

8 get / cup / tea / in / a / You / shop / can / of / the

____.

9 may / home / go / You / now

____.

10 speak / exam / may not / You / this / during

____.

11 I / your / see / passports / May

____?

12 May / cinema / we / today / to / go / the

____?

13 help / the / You / housework / may / me / with

____.

Exercise 1

Can the man jump?	Can the woman hear?	Can the biker fly?

a) Yes, he can.	a) No, she can't.	a) Yes, he can.
b) No, he can't.	b) Yes, she can.	b) No, he can't.
Can the man swim?	Can the cat play?	Can he run?

a) No, he can't.	a) Yes, it can.	a) Yes, he can.
b) Yes, he can.	b) No, it can't.	b) No, he can't.

Exercise 2

1 Marc and Tim are good at the saxophone; they **can** play the saxophone well.
2 You know the answer to the question! You **can** answer the question.
3 Marianne can speak English but she **can't** speak Korean.
4 I am very nervous today! I **can't** sleep.
5 Joseph **can** play basketball very well: he is an excellent basketball player.
6 This test is very difficult; I **can't** answer any of the questions.

Exercise 3

Wir **dürfen** hier drinnen spielen. **Dürfen** wir hier drinnen spielen?	We **can** play in here. **Can** we play in here?
Sie **kann** dein Telefon benutzen. **Kann** sie dein Telefon benutzen?	She **can** use your telephone. **Can** she use your telephone?

Exercise 4

1 go / We / swimming / tomorrow / can
We can go swimming tomorrow.

2 John / speak / Can't / English
Can't John speak English?

3 sugar / Can / the / I / please / have
Can I have the sugar, please?

4 school / to / You / today / go / can't / ill / are / because / you
You can't go to school today because you are ill.

5 TV / She / because / broken / it's / can't / watch
She can't watch TV because it's broken.

6 cook / for / Saturday / they / on / lunch / can / What
What can they cook for lunch on Saturday?

7 get / we / taxi / a / can / Where
Where can we get a taxi?

8 get / cup / tea / in / a / You / shop / can / of / the
You can get a cup of tea in the shop.

9 may / home / go / You / now
You may go home now.

10 speak / exam / may not / You / this / during
You may not speak during this exam.

11 I / your / see / passports / May
May I see your passports?

12 May / cinema / we / today / to / go / the
May we go to the cinema today?

13 help / the / You / housework / may / me / with
You may help me with the housework.

ANSWER KEY ANSWER KEY ANSWER KEY

18 *Mustn't/needn't/don't have to* in negative statements (Verneinungen mit *mustn't/needn't/don't have to*)

1 *Must not/mustn't*

Must not/mustn't bedeutet ein strenges Verbot, also dass jemand etwas keinesfalls tun darf.

Die Form ***must not*** oder ***mustn't*** ist in allen Personen gleich. Nach ***must not/mustn't*** folgt der Infinitiv des Vollverbs (ohne ***to***).

must not/mustn't	
*You **must not** feed a lion. It's dangerous.*	Du **darfst** einen Löwen **nicht** füttern. Es ist gefährlich.
*The thief **mustn't** steal again, otherwise he will have to go to prison.*	Der Dieb **darf nicht** wieder stehlen, sonst muss er ins Gefängnis gehen.
*You **must not** cross the road when the lights are red.*	Du **darfst** die Straße **nicht** überqueren, wenn die Ampel Rot zeigt.

Aufgepasst! ***Must not*** ist im Englischen **nicht** die Verneinung von ***must. Must not*** klingt zwar wie *muss nicht,* darf aber keinesfalls damit verwechselt werden, da sich die Bedeutung des gesamten Satzes dadurch verändert.

2 *Need not/needn't*

Um zu sagen, dass jemand etwas nicht zu tun braucht oder nicht tun muss, benutzt man ***need not*** bzw. ***needn't. Need not*** drückt also aus, dass keine Verpflichtung besteht. Die Form ***need not*** oder ***needn't*** ist in allen Personen gleich. Nach ***need not/needn't*** und ***must not/mustn't*** folgt der Infinitiv des Vollverbs (ohne ***to***).

need not/needn't	
*I **need not** do any homework today. Today's my birthday.*	Ich **brauche** heute **keine** Hausaufgaben zu machen. Heute ist mein Geburtstag.
*You **needn't** learn for the test because you already know everything? Fine!*	Du **brauchst nicht** für den Test zu lernen, weil du schon alles weißt? Toll!

3 *Don't have to/doesn't have to*

Die Verneinung von ***have to*** heißt ***don't have to*** bzw. für die 3. Person Singular ***doesn't have to.*** Man kann auch diese Formen verwenden, um auszudrücken, dass kein Zwang oder keine Notwendigkeit besteht, etwas zu tun. Auch nach ***don't have to/doesn't have to*** folgt direkt das Vollverb (ohne ***to***).

don't have to/doesn't have to	
*You **don't have to** do any homework? You're lucky.*	Du **musst keine** Hausaufgaben machen? Du hast es gut.
*He **doesn't have to** wash his clothes. His mother washes them for him.*	Er **braucht** seine Kleider nicht zu waschen. Seine Mutter wäscht sie für ihn.

EXERCISE 1 Which form is correct: **must not** or **need not?** Underline it.

The teacher tells his class: "We are going to a museum for prehistoric history next week. You *must not/need not* take your schoolbags with you on that day. I will collect the money for the entry fee and the underground on Monday, so you *must not/need not* bring any money with you. On the way from school to the museum you *must not/need not* run away, but you *must not/need not* stay next to me all the time: just stay together in a group. When we arrive at the museum, you can look at everything carefully but you *must not/need not* touch anything. The rules also say you *must not/need not* take any photographs as you can buy postcards. Because there are other people in the museum, you *must not/need not* talk too loud. In the museum, you *must not/need not* run for the same reason, but you *must not/need not* hurry through the museum – we've got lots of time!"

EXERCISE 2 Look at the signs and answer the questions by using **mustn't** or **needn't.**

1 Can I park here?

No, you ______________________________.

2 Can I go straight ahead?

______________________________.

3 Do I have to get off my bicycle here?

______________________________.

4 Can I turn left here?

______________________________.

Exercise 3 Write sentences with these words.

1 isn't / we / take / away, / The / need not / zoo / so / far / bus. / the

____

2 go / if / the / You / better / must / to / feel / you / tomorrow. / doctor / don't

____

3 mustn't / in / the / hot / wash / You / pullover / water.

____

4 to / don't / pay / You / now. / have / cash

____

5 be / 8 pm. / because / film / late / mustn't / for / begins / We / the / it / at

____

6 if / worried / bad / children / Parents / be / get / must / their / marks.

____

7 is / so / needn't / correct / do / her / she / again. / homework / Everything

____

Exercise 4 Choose between **must/need to, mustn't** and **don't/doesn't have to/ needn't** to fill in the gaps.

1 You ______________ talk all the time. I want to listen to the music.

2 We can look after your baby. You ______________ call a babysitter.

3 Your room is full of rubbish. You ______________ tidy it up!

4 If you don't want to, you ______________ come.

5 He ______________ speak to his teacher in such a bad way.

6 We ______________ wait for Bob – he is already at the circus.

7 You are 17 years old. You ______________ buy a ticket.

8 She is only 4 years old. She ______________ buy a ticket.

9 Don't worry about your birthday cake, I'll bake it. You ______________ worry.

10 I ______________ put on a warm coat. It's cold outside.

Exercise 1

The teacher tells his class: "We are going to a museum for prehistoric history next week. You **must not/need not** take your schoolbags with you on that day. I will collect the money for the entry fee and the underground on Monday, so you **must not/need not** bring any money with you. On the way from school to the museum you **must not/need not** run away, but you **must not/need not** stay next to me all the time: just keep together in a group. When we arrive at the museum, you can look at everything carefully but you **must not/need not** touch anything. The rules also say you **must not/need not** take any photographs as you can buy postcards. Because there are other people in the museum, you **must not/need not** talk too loud. In the museum, you **must not/need not** run for the same reason, but you **must not/need not** hurry through the museum – we've got lots of time!"

Exercise 2

1 Can I park here?
No, you **mustn't** park here.

2 Can I go straight ahead?
No, you **mustn't** go straight ahead (but you can turn right or left).

3 Do I have to get off my bicycle here?
No, you **needn't** get off your bicycle here (as this is a path for cyclis and pedestrians).

4 Can I turn left here?
No, you **mustn't** turn left here.

Exercise 3

1 **The zoo isn't far away, so we need not take the bus.**
2 **You must go to the doctor if you don't feel better tomorrow.**
3 **You mustn't wash the pullover in hot water.**
4 **You don't have to pay cash now.**
5 **We mustn't be late for the film because it begins at 8 pm.**
6 **Parents must be worried if their children get bad marks.**
7 **Everything is correct so she needn't do her homework again.**

Exercise 4

1 You **mustn't** talk all the time. I want to listen to the music.
2 We can look after your baby. You **don't have to/needn't** call a babysitter.
3 Your room is full of rubbish. You **must/need to** tidy it up!
4 If you don't want to, you **don't have to/needn't** come.
5 He **mustn't** speak to his teacher in such a bad way.
6 We **don't have to/needn't** wait for Bob – he is already at the circus.
7 You are 17 years old. You **must/need to** buy a ticket.
8 She is only 4 years old. She **doesn't have to/needn't** buy a ticket.
9 Don't worry about your birthday cake, I'll bake it. You **don't have to/needn't** worry.
10 I **must/need to** put on a warm coat. It's cold outside.

19 Articles: definite *(the)* and indefinite *(a/an)* (Bestimmte und unbestimmte Artikel)

Artikel im Englischen werden ähnlich benutzt wie im Deutschen. Sie stehen vor Nomen bzw. vor Adjektiv-Nomen-Kombinationen.
Aber es gibt Besonderheiten bei:

- der ***pronunciation*** *(Aussprache)* von ***the,***
- dem ***definite article*** *(dem bestimmten Artikel),* und
- dem ***spelling*** *(der Schreibweise)* von ***a,*** dem ***indefinite article*** *(dem unbestimmten Artikel).*

1 The definite article *the*: pronunciation

Der ***definite article,*** also ***the,*** bleibt in seiner geschriebenen Form immer gleich, aber die Aussprache ändert sich manchmal von [ðə] zu [ðɪ].
Dabei erklingt [ðə] vor Konsonanten (Mitlauten) und [ðɪ] vor Vokalen (Selbstlauten).

Hier sind einige Beispiele, die du dir anhören kannst:

[ðə]	[ðɪ]
the boy, the cat, the girl, the house, the pencil, the green apple	*the apple, the exercise, the idea, the uncle, the old house*

2 The indefinite article *a/an:* spelling

Der ***indefinite article*** lautet vor Konsonanten ***a,*** vor Vokalen ***an.***

a	an
a *boy,* ***a*** *cat,* ***a*** *girl,* ***a*** *house,* ***a*** *pencil,* ***a*** *nice idea*	***an*** *apple,* ***an*** *exercise,* ***an*** *idea,* ***an*** *uncle,* ***an*** *Indian boy*

Wie man sehen und hören kann, kommt es auf den Anfang des folgenden Wortes an, ob ***the*** bzw. ***a*** verändert werden müssen.

Erklärung: Die Veränderung der beiden Artikel dient dazu, die Aussprache aufeinanderfolgender Wörter einfacher zu machen. Das kannst du selbst ausprobieren: Wenn du ***a*** *car* sagst, kannst du die beiden Wörter beim Sprechen sozusagen ineinander übergehen lassen. Versuche das Gleiche mit einer Kombination aus ***a*** und ***uncle.*** Du wirst feststellen, dass du beim Sprechen nach ***a*** eine kleine Pause machen musst, bevor du ***uncle*** anfängst. Um dieses Problem zu umgehen, wird im Englischen einfach das ***n*** bei ***an*** eingeschoben, und schon geht die Kombination ***an uncle*** flüssig über die Lippen. Das Gleiche gilt für die Lautänderung bei ***the*** von [ðə] zu [ðɪ].

Es geht dabei um den Laut am Anfang des Folgewortes, nicht um die Schreibweise. Es heißt ***an*** *uncle,* weil ***uncle*** in der Aussprache mit [ʌ] anfängt [ʌŋkl], aber bei ***a*** *uniform* ist das anders, da *uniform* beim Sprechen mit [j] beginnt [juːnɪfɔːrm].

Exercise 1 Is it **the** [ðə] or **the** [ðɪ]? Tick the right box.

Terfel is at school today. His favourite teacher is Miss Takes, the (☐ [ðə] ☐ [ðɪ]) English teacher.

Cecily, Steve and Terfel are never late for her class. The (☐ [ðə] ☐ [ðɪ]) best thing is that Miss Takes is always happy. The (☐ [ðə] ☐ [ðɪ]) English book is yellow and blue, but the (☐ [ðə] ☐ [ðɪ]) exercise books for her class are pink! The (☐ [ðə] ☐ [ðɪ]) two pink exercise books are in Terfel's school bag, but the (☐ [ðə] ☐ [ðɪ]) English book is on his desk now. Terfel's folder and his pencil case are on the (☐ [ðə] ☐ [ðɪ]) desk, too. There are a lot of things in it he likes: the (☐ [ðə] ☐ [ðɪ]) nice red pencil and the (☐ [ðə] ☐ [ðɪ]) orange pencils, all the (☐ [ðə] ☐ [ðɪ]) other pens, Terfel's yellow ruler and the (☐ [ðə] ☐ [ðɪ]) rubber.

Now listen to the text. Have you got it right?

Exercise 2 **A** or **an?** Put in the correct form.

Miss Takes is in the classroom now. All the pupils are there, but what is that? There is *an* empty desk. "Where is Steve?" First the pupils have no answer for Miss Takes. But then

Cecily has ____ idea: "I think he must get some things for Mr Beemer, our German teacher." Miss Takes doesn't look very happy, but normally she is never ____ unhappy teacher. "What must he get for Mr Beemer?" – "____ German book, ____ old pen and ____ new pen, ____ map of Germany, ____ exercise book – I think it's Steve's exercise book – and ____ new poster of ____ football team from Germany." Now Miss Takes is very happy again: "It is nice that Steve can help Mr Beemer. He's ____ good boy."

EXERCISE 3 What is the right form of the article? Underline it!

Now Mr Beemer has got all the ([ðə]/[ðɪ]) things and Steve is in the classroom again. Miss Takes has got a/an new question: "What is a/an garage?" Of course, all the pupils know the ([ðə]/[ðɪ]) answer! It's a/an house for a/an car. But why the ([ðə]/[ðɪ]) question?

She starts to tell a / an story about a/an garage. Here it is:

Lunchtime fun

It's Sunday. The Taylors are in the ([ðə]/[ðɪ]) kitchen. Mrs Taylor says:

"Let's have a/an good lunch. Jenny, you set the ([ðə]/[ðɪ]) table. Jason, put the ([ðə]/[ðɪ]) glasses on the ([ðə]/[ðɪ]) table."

Jenny and Jason do these things. Then they sit down next to the ([ðə]/[ðɪ]) door.

Mrs Taylor looks around.

"Where is your father? He isn't here."

Jenny looks at Jason. Then she says:

"Dad is in the ([ðə]/[ðɪ]) garage. It's open. You can find him in the ([ðə]/[ðɪ]) open garage. It's lunchtime for our new red horse, too."

Mrs Taylor calls out:

"We've got a/an what? Are you crazy?" And she runs outside. Mr Taylor comes in: "Where is your mother?"

"Er ... outside," is all Jenny can say, then she and Jason start to laugh. What a/an trick!

The pupils like the ([ðə]/[ðɪ]) funny story. Now Miss Takes gives them a/an job:

"Let's make a / an comic strip from the ([ðə]/[ðɪ]) story! One group takes the ([ðə]/[ðɪ]) beginning of the little story and the ([ðə]/[ðɪ]) other group makes the ([ðə]/[ðɪ]) ending."

The children start to draw the ([ðə]/[ðɪ]) pictures. Then Cecily has got a problem:

"Terfel, can you give me a / an orange pencil, please? I can't find my pencil!" Of course Terfel can help:

"Yes, you can take it out of my pencil case. But it's in the ([ðə]/[ðɪ]) old pencil case in my school bag, not in the ([ðə]/[ðɪ]) new pencil case on my desk."

At the ([ðə]/[ðɪ]) end of Miss Takes' lesson, the pupils can put their comic strip on the wall.

Now you can listen to this text. Have you got it right?

Exercise 1

Terfel is at school today. His favourite teacher is Miss Takes, the [ðɪ] English teacher. Cecily, Steve and Terfel are never late for her class. The [ðə] best thing is that Miss Takes is always happy.
The [ðɪ] English book is yellow and blue, but the [ðɪ] exercise books for her class are pink! The [ðə] two pink exercise books are in Terfel's school bag, but the [ðɪ] English book is on his desk now. Terfel's folder and his pencil case are on the [ðə] desk, too. There are a lot of things in it he likes: the [ðə] nice red pencil and the [ðɪ] orange pencils, all the [ðɪ] other pens, Terfel's yellow ruler and the [ðe] rubber.

Exercise 2

Miss Takes is in the classroom now. All the pupils are there, but what is that? There is **an** empty desk. "Where is Steve?" First the pupils have no answer for Miss Takes. But then Cecily has **an** idea: "I think he must get some things for Mr Beemer, our German teacher." Miss Takes doesn't look very happy, but normally she is never **an** unhappy teacher. "What must he get for Mr Beemer?" –
"**A** German book, **an** old pen and **a** new pen, **a** map of Germany, **an** exercise book – I think it's Steve's exercise book – and **a** new poster of **a** football team from Germany." Now Miss Takes is very happy again: "It is nice that Steve can help Mr Beemer. He's **a** good boy."

Exercise 3

Now Mr Beemer has got all the ([ðə]/[ðɪ]) things and Steve is in the classroom again. Miss Takes has got a/an new question: "What is a/an garage?" Of course, all the pupils know the ([ðə]/[ðɪ]) answer! It's a/an house for a/an car. But why the ([ðə]/[ðɪ]) question?
She starts to tell a/an story about a/an garage. Here it is:

Lunchtime fun

It's Sunday. The Taylors are in the ([ðə]/[ðɪ]) kitchen. Mrs Taylor says:
"Let's have a/an good lunch. Jenny, you set the ([ðə]/[ðɪ]) table. Jason, put the ([ðə]/[ðɪ]) glasses on the ([ðə]/[ðɪ]) table."
Jenny and Jason do these things. Then they sit down next to the ([ðə]/[ðɪ]) door. Mrs Taylor looks around.
"Where is your father? He isn't here."
Jenny looks at Jason. Then she says:
"Dad is in the ([ðə]/[ðɪ]) garage. It's open. You can find him in the ([ðə]/[ðɪ]) open garage. It's lunchtime for our new red horse, too." Mrs Taylor calls out:
"We've got a/an what? Are you crazy?"
And she runs outside. Mr Taylor comes in:
"Where is your mother?"
"Er ... outside," is all Jenny can say, then she and Jason start to laugh. What a/an trick!

The pupils like the ([ðə]/[ðɪ]) funny story. Now Miss Takes gives them a/an job:
"Let's make a/an comic strip from the ([ðə]/[ðɪ]) story! One group takes the ([ðə]/[ðɪ]) beginning of the little story and the ([ðə]/[ðɪ]) other group makes the ([ðə]/[ðɪ]) ending."
The children start to draw the ([ðə]/[ðɪ]) pictures. Then Cecily has got a problem:
"Terfel, can you give me a/an orange pencil, please? I can't find my pencil!"
Of course Terfel can help:
"Yes, you can take it out of my pencil case. But it's in the ([ðə]/[ðɪ]) old pencil case in my school bag, not in the ([ðə]/[ðɪ]) new pencil case on my desk."
At the ([ðə]/[ðɪ]) end of Miss Takes' lesson, the pupils can put their comic strip on the wall.

ANSWER KEY ANSWER KEY ANSWER KEY

20 Personal pronouns as (direct/indirect) objects (Personalpronomen als direkte/indirekte Objektpronomen)

Die ***personal pronouns*** *(Personalpronomen)* können im Satz anstelle von Objekten stehen. Dann heißen sie ***Objektpronomen*** und stehen in der Objektform.

Objektpronomen können ***indirect objects*** ersetzen (Dativobjekte, Frage: „Wem/Was?"):

- *Ray can help **the teacher.** → Ray can help **him.*** (Hier steht ***him*** als indirektes Objektpronomen.)

Objektpronomen können auch ***direct objects*** ersetzen (Akkusativobjekte, Frage: „Wen/Was?"):

- *Claire likes **computers.** → Claire likes **them.*** (Hier steht ***them*** als direktes Objektpronomen.)

Direkte und indirekte Objektpronomen unterscheiden sich im Englischen in ihrer Form nicht voneinander.

1 Personal pronouns as indirect objects

indirect object	indirektes Objektpronomen	
me	mir	*She is helping **me** with my homework.*
you	dir, Ihnen	*Can I talk to **you?***
him/her	ihm/ihr	*Peter is writing **him/her** a letter.*
it	es, ihm, ihr (wenn Sache)	*Listen to **it!***
us	uns	*They cannot help **us.***
you	euch, Ihnen	*Can we bring **you** something to drink?*
them	ihnen	*Please help **them!***

2 Personal pronouns as direct object

direct object	direktes Objektpronomen	
me	mich	*Can't she see **me?***
you	dich, Sie	*They want to meet **you** at 7 o'clock.*
him/her	ihn/sie	*Do you know **him/her?***
it	es, ihn, sie (wenn Sache)	*He is reading **it.***
us	uns	*I hope he doesn't see **us.***
you	euch, Sie	*They aren't watching **you.***
them	sie	*We cannot find **them.***

3 Exceptions: same forms

Das Pronomen ***her*** kann entweder Objektpronomen *(I help **her**.)* oder Possessivbegleiter *(Peter is **her** friend.)* sein.

Das Pronomen ***you*** kann Subjektpronomen sein (also für das Subjekt stehen): ***You** can help Peter.* Es kann aber auch Objektpronomen sein: *Peter can help **you.*** (indirektes Objekt) oder *Peter likes **you.*** (direktes Objekt).

EXERCISE 1 Underline the object pronouns. Then find out: is the underlined pronoun an **indirect** or a **direct object?**

1 My friend Jessica is really nice. She always helps *me* with my homework.

me = indirect object

2 They never listen to us.

____

3 This is a great book. You must read it.

____

4 There she is. I can see her.

____

5 We can write them a letter to say thank you for the present.

____

6 My teacher knows me very well. He knows that I am sometimes lazy.

____

7 This dog is always angry. I don't like it very much.

____

EXERCISE 2 Underline the correct solution.

I eat a lot of chocolate.I eat *them/it/you* every day.
We are hungry! Can you give *us/our/her* something to eat, please?
Where is Timmy? I cannot find *his/him/they.*
These CDs are really good. Let's buy *us/it/them.*
Excuse me, I'm new in this town. Can you tell *my/me/I* the way to the church, please?
Jennifer is not here. Her friend is playing tennis with *her/him/their.*
Here is my new book. I want to read *him/it/she* this afternoon.
Harry is not at home. Please call *us/he/him* on his mobile.
Aunt Margaret is coming today. We have to meet *her/she/you* at the airport at 6.40 pm.
Children, speak louder, please! I cannot hear *you/they/she.*
Can you give *it/they/me* this magazine, please? Thank you!
There is a new boy in class. Do you know *her/him/he?*
John and Dexter are in town. Let's meet *them/us/their* this evening.
I don't know where it is. I can't see *it/her/me.*
Do you want to go shopping with *us/they/she?*

EXERCISE 3 Find the correct translation for the **object pronouns.**

Nie ruft sie **mich** an! Immer muss ich **sie** anrufen!	*me, her*
Bitte hilf **ihm** bei seinen Hausaufgaben.	
Kannst du **ihnen** die Stadt zeigen? Sie kennen **sie** nicht.	
Wie lange willst du **es** noch suchen? Du wirst **es** nicht finden.	
Wann wirst du **uns** wieder schreiben?	
Das Paket liegt bei der Post. Wir müssen **es** bald abholen.	
Sarah ist bei ihrer Freundin. Sie bringt **ihr** Blumen.	

EXERCISE 4 Complete the dialogue between Sarah and her mother with the correct **object pronouns.**

Sarah's mother: "Sarah! Where are you? I cannot find *you.*"

Sarah: "I'm in my room, Mum! Do you remember *(= sich erinnern an)* Martin? I'm writing _______ a letter."

Sarah's mother: "Oh, yes, I remember Martin and his brother. They are very nice. I like _______ very much. Do you know their mother, too?"

Sarah: "Yes, I know _______ but I don't think that she likes _______. She is not very nice to _______."

Sarah's mother: "Sarah, your sister needs your help. Can you give _______ your English book?"

Sarah: "I don't want to help _______ and I don't want to give _______ to her!"

Sarah's mother: "Please be nice to _______ and help _______! She really needs _______ (= the English book) to do her homework. Your sister always helps _______ when you have a problem!"

Sarah: "OK, if you promise to go shopping with _______ and buy _______ a new pair of jeans. My friends Annabel and Maple are already in the shopping centre. Maybe we can meet _______ there."

Sarah's mother: "That's a good idea."

Exercise 1

1 My friend Jessica is really nice.
She always helps **me** with my homework. **me = indirect object**
2 They never listen to **us.** **us = indirect object**
3 This is a great book. You must read **it.** **it = direct object**
4 There she is. I can see **her.** **her = direct object**
5 We can write **them** a letter to say thank you for the present.
them = indirect object
6 My teacher knows **me** very well. He knows that I am sometimes lazy.
me = direct object
7 This dog is always angry. I don't like **it** very much. **it = direct object**

Exercise 2

I eat a lot of chocolate. I eat *them*/**it**/*you* every day.
We are hungry! Can you give **us**/*our*/*her* something to eat, please?
Where is Timmy? I cannot find *his*/**him**/*they*.
These CDs are really good. Let's buy *us*/*it*/**them.**
Excuse me, I'm new in this town. Can you tell my/**me**/I the way to the church, please?
Jennifer is not here. Her friend is playing tennis with **her**/*him*/*their*.
Here is my new book. I want to read *him*/**it**/*she* this afternoon.
Harry is not at home. Please call *us*/*he*/**him** on his mobile.
Aunt Margaret is coming today. We have to meet **her**/*she*/*you* at the airport at 6.40 pm.
Children, speak louder, please! I cannot hear **you**/*they*/*she*.
Can you give *it*/*they*/**me** this magazine, please? Thank you.
There is a new boy in class. Do you know *her*/**him**/*he?*
John and Dexter are in town. Let's meet **them**/*us*/*their* this evening.
I don't know where it is. I can't see **it**/*her*/*me*.
Do you want to go shopping with **us**/*they*/*she?*

Exercise 3

Nie ruft sie **mich** an! Immer muss ich **sie** anrufen!	**me, her**
Bitte hilf **ihm** bei seinen Hausaufgaben.	**him**
Kannst du **ihnen** die Stadt zeigen? Sie kennen **sie** nicht!	**them, it**
Wie lange willst du **es** noch suchen? Du wirst **es** nicht finden!	**it, it**
Wann wirst du **uns** wieder schreiben?	**us**
Das Paket liegt bei der Post. Wir müssen **es** bald abholen.	**it**
Sarah ist bei ihrer Freundin. Sie bringt **ihr** Blumen.	**her**

Exercise 4

Sarah's mother: "Sarah! Where are you? I cannot find **you.**"
Sarah: "I'm in my room, Mum! Do you remember (= sich erinnern an) Martin? I'm writing **him** a letter."
Sarah's mother: "Oh, yes, I remember Martin and his brother. They are very nice. I like **them** very much. Do you know their mother, too?"
Sarah: "Yes, I know **her** but I don't think that she likes **me.** She is not very nice to **me.**"
Sarah's mother: "Sarah, your sister needs your help. Can you give **her** your English book?"
Sarah: "I don't want to help **her** and I don't want to give **it** to her!"
Sarah's mother: "Please be nice to **her** and help **her!** She really needs **it** (= the English book) to do her homework. Your sister always helps **you** when you have a problem!"
Sarah: "OK, if you promise to go shopping with **me** and buy **me** a new pair of jeans. My friends Annabel and Maple are already in the shopping centre. Maybe we can meet **them** there."
Sarah's mother: "That's a good idea."

ANSWER KEY ANSWER KEY ANSWER KEY

21 Numbers (Zahlen)

1 Numbers from 0 – 20

Die Zahl **0** heißt im Englischen ***zero*** oder auch ***o.*** Die weiteren Zahlen bis 20 sind.

1	***one***	11	***eleven***
2	***two***	12	***twelve***
3	***three***	13	***thirteen***
4	***four***	14	***fourteen***
5	***five***	15	***fifteen***
6	***six***	16	***sixteen***
7	***seven***	17	***seventeen***
8	***eight***	18	***eighteen***
9	***nine***	19	***nineteen***
10	***ten***	20	***twenty***

Die Zahlen von 1 – 20 werden **in einem Wort** geschrieben.

2 Numbers from 21–100

Ab der Zahl 21 werden die Zehner mit einem **Bindestrich** vor die Einer gestellt.

21	***twenty-one***	29	***twenty-nine***
22	***twenty-two***	30	***thirty***
23	***twenty-three***	40	***forty***
24	***twenty-four***	50	***fifty***
25	***twenty-five***	60	***sixty***
26	***twenty-six***	70	***seventy***
27	***twenty-seven***	80	***eighty***
28	***twenty-eight***	90	***ninety***

Besonders aufpassen muss man bei der Schreibweise von ***five, fifteen, fifty*** und ***four, forty.*** Für die Zahl 100 sagt man im Englischen ***a hundred*** oder ***one hundred.***

3 Numbers higher than 100

Bei Zahlen, die über 100 und unter 1000 liegen, setzt man die Zahl 1-9 vor das Wort ***hundred.*** Vor die folgende Zahl wird das Wort ***and*** gesetzt.

111	***one hundred and eleven***
551	***five hundred and fifty-one***
625	***six hundred and twenty-five***
713	***seven hundred and thirteen***

Die Zahl 1000 heißt auf Englisch ***a thousand*** oder ***one thousand.***
Die entsprechende Zahl der Tausender wird vor das Wort ***thousand*** gesetzt.

1,111	***one thousand one hundred and eleven***
7,551	***seven thousand five hundred and fifty-one***

Tausender trennt man im Englischen durch ein Komma. 1 Million heißt im Englischen ***a*** oder ***one million.*** Für 1 Milliarde sagt man auf Englisch ***a*** oder ***one billion.***

Exercise 1 Write down the numbers in English (in words).

746 *seven hundred and forty-six*

13 ________________

555 ________________

2,315 ________________

25,711 ________________

699 ________________

Exercise 2 What are these numbers? Write them down (in words).

eynsevt-ehter	*seventy-three*	xstyi-eon	
nlveee		tryhti-owt	
yttnew-einn		ghtiye-hgtie	
tftiy-vfei		rzoe	
etnnneie		nntyie-xsi	

Exercise 3 Are you good at maths? Match the sums and the calculations. Then write down the correct result in English (in words) and cross out the correct sum in brackets.

1 13 + 25 = *thirty-eight* (148)

2 101 – 47 = ________________ (167)

3 19 + 129 = ________________ (20)

4 379 – 82 = ________________ (54)

5 95 + 216 = ________________ ~~(38)~~

6 122 + 45 = ________________ (314)

7 2,014 – 601 = ________________ (311)

8 44 – 17 = ________________ (0)

9 515 + 126 = ________________ (27)

10 295 + 19 = ________________ (641)

11 132 – 55 – 77 = ________________ (1,413)

12 177 – 157 = ________________ (297)

Exercise 4 Which number is missing? Write it down (in words).

7 + ??? + 28 = 49 *fourteen*

126 - 39 -??? = 50 ______

??? + 1,248 = 2,515 ______

99 - 58 + 207 = ??? ______

13 + 179 + ??? = 218 ______

138 - ??? - 72 + 21 = 87 ______

??? - 11 + 91 - 108 = 3,333 ______

180 + 64 - 172 = ??? ______

27 + 418 - ??? = 132 ______

1,106 - 842 + ??? = 556 ______

Exercise 5 Work out the correct result and write it down (in words).

55 : 11 =	*five*
7 x 6 =	
28 : 4 =	
125 : 5 =	
91 : 7 =	
13 x 9 =	
21 x 4 =	
56 : 7 =	
144 : 12 =	

Exercise 1

746	**seven hundred and forty-six**
13	**thirteen**
555	**five hundred and fifty-five**
2,315	**two thousand three hundred and fifteen**
25,711	**twenty-five thousand seven hundred and eleven**
699	**six hundred and ninety-nine**

Exercise 2

eynsevt-ehter	**seventy-three**	xstyi-eon	**sixty-one**
nlveee	**eleven**	tryhti-owt	**thirty-two**
yttnew-einn	**twenty-nine**	ghtiye-hgtie	**eighty-eight**
tftiy-vfei	**fifty-five**	rzoe	**zero**
etnnneie	**nineteen**	nntyie-xsi	**ninety-six**

Exercise 3

38	**thirty-eight**
54	**fifty-four**
148	**one hundred and forty-eight**
297	**two hundred and ninety-seven**
311	**three hundred and eleven**
167	**one hundred and sixty-seven**
1,413	**one thousand four hundred and thirteen**
27	**twenty-seven**
641	**six hundred and forty-one**
314	**three hundred and fourteen**
0	**zero**
20	**twenty**

Exercise 4

7 + ??? + 28 = 49 **fourteen**
126 – 39 – ??? = 50 **thirty-seven**
??? + 1,248 = 2,515 **one thousand two hundred and sixty-seven**
99 – 58 + 207 = ??? **two hundred and forty-eight**
13 + 179 + ??? = 218 **twenty-six**
138 – ??? – 72 + 21 = 87 **zero**
??? – 11 + 91 – 108 = 3,333 **three thousand three hundred and sixty-one**
180 + 64 – 172 = ??? **seventy-two**
27 + 418 – ??? = 132 **three hundred and thirteen**
1,106 – 842 + ??? = 556 **two hundred and ninety-two**

Exercise 5

55 : 11 =	**five**
7 x 6 =	**forty-two**
28 : 4 =	**seven**
125 : 5 =	**twenty-five**
91 : 7 =	**thirteen**
13 x 9 =	**one hundred and seventeen**
21 x 4 =	**eighty-four**
56 : 7 =	**eight**
144 : 12 =	**twelve**

ANSWER KEY ANSWER KEY ANSWER KEY

Can and *must* in statements and *yes/no* questions

EXERCISE 1 Fill in **can** or **must.**

Mum: "Linda, _______ you help me in the kitchen?"

Linda: "Sorry Mum, but I _______ do my homework! I _______ finish it today."

Mum: "But you _______ help me now and you _______ do your homework later! Your sister _______ do her homework, too, and your father _______ work in the garden."

Linda: "Okay Mum, I _______ help you. But then, I _______ do some exercises for school. _______ you help me with them?"

Mum: "Yes, I _______ help you with the exercises."

Linda: "Great! Thank you, Mum."

11 P

Have to/has to: statements and questions

EXERCISE 2 Write down what Michael and his sister Judy have to do. Use **have to/has to.**

Michael	Judy
take the dog for a walk | make his bed	do her homework | write a letter to Aunt Betty
Michael and Judy	
make a birthday cake for their father | clean the garage	

1 Michael ____.

2 He ____.

3 Judy ____.

4 She ____.

5 Michael and Judy ____.

6 They ____.

6 P

EXERCISE 3 Fill in the blanks with a form of **to have to.**

1 Peter _______________ give me this book back. I need it for school!

2 Come on, let's go to the cinema. We _______________ see this new film.

3 Cindy and Sarah, you _______________ help me in the kitchen!

4 I cannot go shopping with you, I _______________ do my homework.

5 Jessica _____________ take her dog for a walk.

6 All the pupils _____________ do these exercises.

7 You _____________ feed your hamster.

8 Do we _____________ buy a present for our mother? Of course we do, it's her birthday!

9 Marc and Timmy _____________ tidy up their rooms.

10 Do you _____________ visit your grandma?

10 P

Can/can't

EXERCISE 4 Listen carefully to the phone call between Jenny and Lisa and fill in the blanks with **can** or **can't.**

Lisa: "Hi Jenny! This is Lisa! ________ you hear me?"

Jenny: "Hi Lisa! Of course, I ________ hear you! Where are you?"

Lisa: "I am in the travel agency with my parents! Jenny, ________ I ask you a question: ________ you go to England with me next summer? We ________ visit my grandparents near Birmingham. They ________ come to us, because they have a farm and they ________ leave their animals alone."

Jenny: "Oh, I am very sorry, but I ________. I must go to Italy with my parents. I ________ tell them that I'm not coming. But maybe we ________ go and visit your grandparents in the November holidays?"

Lisa: "Okay, that's a good idea. I ________ talk to my parents. Maybe we ________ change our plans. But I ________ promise you anything. ________ you call me this evening?"

Jenny: "No, I ________, because I am going to the cinema. But I ________ call you tomorrow. Okay?"

Lisa: "Okay. Goodbye, Jenny!"

16 P

Mustn't/needn't/don't have to in negative statements

EXERCISE 5 **Mustn't** or **don't have to/doesn't have to?**

	mustn't	don't have to	doesn't have to
Thank you, but you **???** help me.			
I **???** go to England to learn English. I can do it at home.			
You **???** cry. If you cry, this makes everybody sad.			
My father **???** work today, so he can go swimming with us.			
I will show you my picture, but you **???** laugh.			
Sarah **???** go to bed at 8 pm. She can watch TV until 9 pm.			
You **???** go shopping, we have everything at home.			
All the pupils like Saturdays because they **???** go to school.			
Our teacher is already waiting for us. We **???** be late.			

9 P

EXERCISE 6 Translate the sentences into English.

1 Du brauchst mir nicht zu helfen. Ich kann es alleine *(= by myself)* machen.

____. 5 P

2 Wir dürfen nicht darüber reden.

____. 5 P

3 Du brauchst dir keine Sorgen zu machen.

____. 5 P

4 Es ist Sonntag. Clara und John müssen heute nicht in die Schule gehen.

____. 7 P

5 Müsst ihr nicht eure Hausaufgaben machen?

____? 5 P

6 Sie brauchen nicht ins Einkaufszentrum zu gehen.

____. 5 P

7 Alex muss seinem Vater nicht helfen.

____. 5 P

8 Ich darf nicht vergessen ihn anzurufen.

____. 5 P

✓ ↩ ?

9 Muss er nicht mit seinem Hund spazieren gehen?

____? 5 P

10 Mr Miller, Sie brauchen mir den Weg nicht zu zeigen.

____. 5 P

Articles: definite *(the)* and indefinite *(a/an)*

EXERCISE 7 Fill in **a, an** or **the.**

1 Mrs Bluemoon is _____ good teacher. I think she is _____ best teacher in our school.

2 Let's go to the cinema! - That's _____ good idea!

3 Is this the picture of _____ dog or _____ cat? It is the picture of a cat, silly!

4 This is our classroom. It is _____ very big room and it has _____ new blackboard, but _____ old computer.

5 Marc is _____ eleven-year-old boy. He is _____ very nice boy and he lives in _____ beautiful house with his family.

6 _____ Simpsons are our neighbours. _____ Millers don't live here anymore.

7 I am looking for _____ black folder. Where is it?

8 That is not _____ answer, that is _____ question!

9 On my desk, there is _____ exercise book and _____ yellow ruler. But _____ English textbook is not there.

10 That's _____ very old book. 10 P

Personal pronouns as *(direct/indirect)* objects

EXERCISE 8 Underline the correct form of the **pronoun.**

1 This is Jenny, my best friend. I really like *them / her / she.*

2 Where are they? I cannot see *their / they / them.*

3 Let's go to the zoo! Can you come with *our / we / us?*

4 Help *me / I / you,* please! I cannot do *they / it / me* alone!

5 Where is my folder? I cannot find *it* / *him* / *them!*

6 Please, call David and tell *he* / *his* / *him* that I want to meet *him* / *them* / *he* at 3 pm.

7 You can go with *she* / *her* / *they* if you want to.

8 I don't know *them* / *they* / *we*. Are they new here?

9 Please show *I* / *we* / *me* the way to the castle.

11 P

Exercise 9 Translate and write down only the **indirect** or **direct object pronoun.**

1 Ich habe es schon gelesen. ________________

2 Sie können mich nicht finden. ________________

3 Meine Mutter hat uns bei unseren Hausaufgaben geholfen. ________________

4 Willst du sie (= deine Freundin) wirklich suchen? ________________

5 Das hast du mir nicht gezeigt. ________________

6 Er hat ihn leicht verletzt. ________________

7 Sie möchten nicht mit ihnen spielen. ________________

8 Seine Schwester sieht ihn, aber sie hört ihn nicht. ________ ________ ________

9 Hast du sie (= die Karte) schon geschrieben? ________________

10 P

Numbers

Exercise 10 Write down the numbers as words.

189 ____

2,337 ____

10,764 ____

1 000 000 ____

1 000 000 000 ____

5 P

Auswertung Trage rechts deine Gesamtpunktzahl ein und vergleiche.

☺ 140 – 106 points	😐 105 – 71 points	☹ 70 – 0 points

TOTAL SCORE 140

Exercise 1

can | must | must | can – can | must – must | can | must | Can | can

Exercise 2

1 Michael **has to** take the dog for a walk. 2 He **has to** make his bed. 3 Judy **has to** do her homework. 4 She **has to** write a letter to Aunt Betty. 5 Michael and Judy **have to** make a birthday cake for their father. 6 They **have to** clean the garage.

Exercise 3

1 Peter **has to** give me this book back. I need it for school!
2 Come on, let's go to the cinema. We **have to** see this new film.
3 Cindy and Sarah, you **have to** help me in the kitchen!
4 I cannot go shopping with you, I **have to** do my homework.
5 Jessica **has to** take her dog for a walk.
6 All the pupils **have to** do these exercises.
7 You **have to** feed your hamster.
8 Do we **have to** buy a present for our mother? Of course we do, it's her birthday!
9 Marc and Timmy **have to** tidy up their rooms.
10 Do you **have to** visit your grandma?

Exercise 4 Can | can | can | can | can | can't – can't | can't | can't | can | can | can | can't | Can | can't | can

Exercise 5

Thank you, but you **don't have to** help me.
I **don't have to go to** England to learn English. I can do it at home.
You **mustn't** cry. If you cry, this makes everybody sad.
My father **doesn't have to** work today, so he can go swimming with us.
I will show you my picture, but you **mustn't** laugh.
Sarah **doesn't have to** go to bed at 8 pm. She can watch TV until 9 pm.
You **don't have to** go shopping, we have everything at home.
All the pupils like Saturdays because they **don't have to** go to school.
Our teacher is already waiting for us. We **mustn't** be late.

Exercise 6

1 You **don't have to (needn't)** help me. I can do it by myself.
2 We **mustn't** talk about it.
3 You **don't have to (needn't)** worry.
4 It's Sunday. Clara and John **don't have to (needn't)** go to school today.
5 **Don't** you **have to** do your homework?
6 They **don't have to (needn't)** go to the shopping centre.
7 Alex **doesn't have to (needn't)** help his father.
8 I **mustn't** forget to call him.
9 **Doesn't** he **have to** take his dog for a walk?
10 Mr Miller, you **don't have to (needn't)** show me the way.

Exercise 7

1 a | the 2 a 3 a – a 4 a – a – an 5 an | a – a
6 The | The 7 the 8 an – a 9 an – a | the 10 a

Exercise 8

1 her 2 them 3 us 4 me | it 5 it
6 him – him 7 her 8 them 9 me

Exercise 9 1 it 2 me 3 us 4 her 5 me 6 him 7 them
8 him – him 9 it

Exercise 10

one hundred and eighty-nine | two thousand three hundred and thirty-seven | ten thousand seven hundred and sixty-four | a (one) million | a (one) billion

22 The present progressive form (Die Verlaufsform des Präsens)

Mit dem ***present progressive*** *(Verlaufsform des Präsens)* drückt man aus,
- dass jemand etwas gerade tut.
- dass ein Vorgang ***in progress*** ist *(gerade abläuft)* und noch nicht abgeschlossen wurde.

1 Form

Das ***present progressive*** wird gebildet aus:

einer Form von ***to be:*** ***am/is/are***	+	Infinitiv des Verbs + ***-ing***

Auch im ***present progressive*** gibt es ***long forms*** und ***short forms:***

	long forms		short forms		
singular	*I* ***am***	***playing*** a song.	*I'**m***	***playing*** a song.	singular
	You ***are***		*You'**re***		
	He / She / It ***is***		*He / She / It'**s***		
plural	*We* ***are***		*We'**re***		plural
	You ***are***		*You'**re***		
	They ***are***		*They'**re***		

2 Spelling

Für die Schreibweise ohne **-e** gibt es einen Merkreim:
Endet ein Verb auf ein ***stummes -e,***
fällt es bei ***-ing*** weg, oh je.

- *writ* ***-e*** → *Sissy is **writ**ing a letter.* *bak* ***-e*** → *Sissy is **bak**ing a cake.*

Ist der **Vokal** im Verb **allein** und **kurz,**
ist uns die Schreibung gar nicht schnurz,
denn kommt ein ***-ing*** dazu,
wird der letzte **Konsonant verdoppelt** im Nu.

- sit ***+ t*** → *Sissy is si**tt**ing next to Bill.* run ***+ n*** → *Sissy is ru**nn**ing around.*

Aufgepasst bei Übersetzungen:

Das ***present progressive*** ist 'ne ***englische Zeit,***
die man im Deutschen suchen kann weit und breit,
es gibt sie nicht und drum wird sie ersetzt,
mit ***gerade, im Augenblick*** oder ***jetzt.***

*Sissy **is drawing** a picture.*	Sissy malt **gerade in diesem Moment** ein Bild.
*Sissy and Bill **are singing** a song.*	Sissy und Bill singen **gerade** ein Lied.

EXERCISE 1 What are Sissy and Bill doing? Connect the sentences. Pay attention to **long forms** and **short forms.**

Sissy and Bill	**am**	reading a book. It is her favourite book.
Sissy: "I	**'m**	listening to music. It is his favourite song.
Bill	**are**	singing a song. They like it a lot.
Sissy	**'re**	dancing and I'm playing the piano."
Sissy and Bill: "We	**is**	doing my homework."
Bill: "Sissy, you	**'s**	playing cards. It's our favourite card game."

EXERCISE 2 Sissy's birthday party. Write sentences in the **present progressive.**

1 to sing / Sissy's friends / a birthday song

____.

2 a present / Bill / for Sissy / to hold

____.

3 to laugh / everybody

____.

4 the birthday cake / Buddy, the dog, / to eat

____.

EXERCISE 3 A Sunday afternoon with Sissy and Bill. Find the differences, number them and write them down.

1

2

3

4

1 *In the picture on the left a boy ...*

2

3

4

Exercise 4 Use the words in the speech bubbles and write down Sissy's excuses *(= Ausreden)*. Pay attention to the **irregular forms of the present progressive.**

Bill: "Hey, Sissy, can you help me, please?"

Sissy: "Sorry Bill, but *I'm making dinner."*

"Sorry Bill, but ______."

"______."

"______."

"______."

"______."

Exercise 1

Sissy and Bill are singing a song. They like it a lot.
Sissy: "I'm doing my homework."
Bill is listening to music. It is his favourite song.
Sissy is reading a book. It's her favourite book.
Sissy and Bill: "We're playing cards. It's our favourite card game."
Bill: "Sissy, you're dancing, and I'm playing the piano."

Exercise 2

1 **Sissy's friends are singing a birthday song.**
2 **Bill is holding a present for Sissy.**
3 **Everybody is laughing.**
4 **Buddy, the dog, is eating the birthday cake.**

Exercise 3

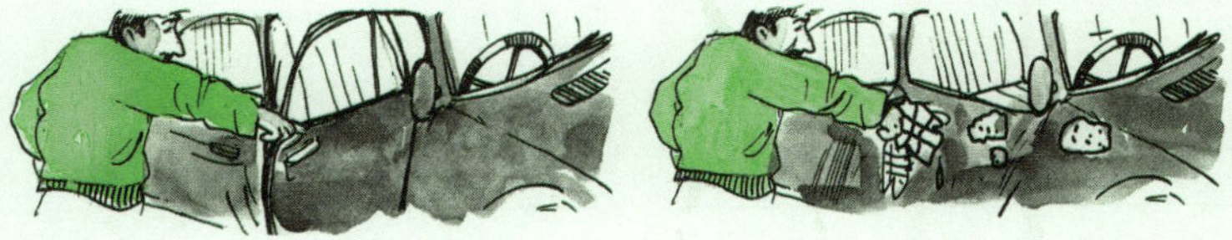

Lösungsbeispiele:

1 In the picture on the left a boy **is sleeping** and in the picture on the right he **is reading** a book in the grass.
2 In the picture on the left the two girls **are looking** into the window and in the picture on the right they **are talking** to each other.
3 In the picture on the left the old woman **is coming** out of the shop and in the picture on the right she **is going** into the shop.
4 In the picture on the left the man **is opening** the car door and in the picture on the right he **is cleaning** the car.

Exercise 4

Lösungsbeispiele:

Sissy: "Sorry Bill, but **I'm making dinner.**"
"Sorry Bill, but **I'm writing a love letter.**"
"Sorry Bill, but **I'm using the computer.**"
"Sorry Bill, but **I'm phoning my friend Rita.**"
"Sorry Bill, but **I'm setting the table.**"
"Sorry Bill, but **I'm sitting in front of the TV.**"

23 The present progressive form in negatives and questions (Die Verlaufsform des Präsens in Verneinungen und Fragen)

1 Negative statements

Verneinte Aussagen im ***present progressive*** *(Verlaufsform des Präsens)* werden gebildet aus:

einer *verneinten Form* von ***to be***	+	Infinitiv des Verbs + ***-ing***

Auch hier gibt es ***long forms*** *(Langformen)* und ***short forms*** *(Kurzformen):*

	long forms		short forms		
singular	*I **am not***	***playing*** a song.	*I'**m not***	***playing*** a song.	singular
	*You **are not***		*You **aren't***		
	*He/She/It **is not***		*He / She / It **isn't***		
plural	*We **are not***		*We **aren't***		plural
	*You **are not***		*You **aren't***		
	*They **are not***		*They **aren't***		

2 The present progressive in questions and short answers

Bei Fragen im ***present progressive*** werden – genauso wie im Deutschen – ***subject*** und ***verb*** miteinander vertauscht. Um nicht unhöflich zu sein, antwortet man im Englischen nicht nur mit ***Yes/No,*** sondern meist mit einer ***short answer*** *(Kurzantwort).*

Sissy **spielt gerade** Karten.	*Sissy **is** playing cards.*
Spielt Sissy **gerade** Karten?	***Is*** *Sissy playing cards?*
Ja./Nein.	***Yes, she is./No, she isn't.***

In positiven Antworten verwendet man immer die ***long form.***

Fragt man danach, **was** eine Person gerade tut, steht das **question word** *(Fragewort),* zum Beispiel ***what,*** an erster Stelle und das Verb ***to be*** an zweiter Stelle.

Singular

- ***What am** I **doing?***
- ***What are** you **doing?***
- ***What is** he/she/it **doing?***

Plural

- ***What are** we **doing?***
- ***What are** you **doing?***
- ***What are** they **doing?***

Exercise 1 Sissy and Bill are on holidays. Write down what they **aren't doing.**

1 getting up / isn't / Sissy / At 6.30 am

At 6.30 am Sissy ______________________________.

2 she / At 7.00 am / having / breakfast / isn't

______________________________.

3 walking / At 7.30 am / aren't / to school / Sissy and her friend Bill

______________________________.

4 At 7.45 am Sissy says: " 'm not / my Maths homework / taking out / I "

"______________________________"

5 At 7.46 am Sissy says: " my homework / you / copying / aren't / right now "

"Haha, Bill, ______________________________."

6 At 8.00 am Sissy and Bill say: "saying / to our Maths teacher / we / Good morning / aren't "

"______________________________"

Exercise 2 Describe the pictures and write down what Sissy **is/isn't doing.**

~~to phone Rita~~ / to send a text message

1 *Sissy isn't phoning Rita.*

She ______________________________

~~to drink orange juice~~ / to eat chocolate

2 ______________________________

____

~~to pull the door~~ / to push it

3 ______________________________

____

~~to cry~~ / to laugh

4 ______________________________

____

Exercise 3 Sissy's mobile phone isn't working. Correct her text message to Rita.

____

____

____

____

____

____

____

Exercise 4 What **is she/are they doing?** Ask questions about the actions and answer them. Use the verbs in the boxes.

to play

to eat

to open

to give

to read

to watch

What is Sissy doing? – She is ______________________________

____

____

____

____

Exercise 1

At 6.30 am Sissy isn't getting up.
At 7.00 am she isn't having breakfast.
At 7.30 am Sissy and her friend Bill aren't walking to school.
At 7.45 am Sissy says: "I'm not taking out my Maths homework."
At 7.46 am Sissy says: "Haha, Bill, you aren't copying my homework right now."
At 8.00 am Sissy and Bill say: "We aren't saying Good morning to our Maths teacher."

Exercise 2

1 Sissy isn't phoning Rita.
She is sending her a text message.

2 Sissy isn't drinking orange juice.
She is eating chocolate.

3 Sissy isn't pulling the door.
She is pushing it.

4 Sissy isn't crying.
She is laughing.

Exercise 3

Hi Rita, how are you doing?
I'm standing in front of the shopping centre and I'm waiting for you and Bill.
Where are you? Are you at home eating ice cream, or are you coming? It's raining and it's very cold. Why is it taking you so long? I'm not smiling anymore!
See you, Sissy.

Exercise 4

What is Sissy doing? – She is opening the door.
What is grandma doing? – She is reading a book.
What is grandpa doing? – He is giving grandma a cup of tea.
What are Sissy's mum and dad doing? – They are watching TV.
What is the cat doing? – It is playing with a pen.
What are the mice doing? – They are eating all the cheese.

24 The simple present (Das einfache Präsens)

Das ***simple present*** *(einfaches Präsens)* zeigt an,

- dass etwas in der Gegenwart regelmäßig oder normalerweise geschieht: *On Mondays **I go** home from school late in the afternoon.*
- dass etwas im Allgemeinen wahr ist: *When **it rains,** the streets get wet.*
- dass verschiedene Dinge hintereinander geschehen: *Cecily **gets up,** then she **has** breakfast, after that she **goes** to school.*

1 Forms of the simple present

Das ***simple present*** lässt sich sehr einfach bilden: Man nimmt den Infinitiv des Verbs. Das ist die Form, in der das Verb im Vokabelteil des Englischbuchs steht, aber ohne das ***to.*** Diese Regel gilt für alle Formen außer für die 3. Person Singular: *I/you/we/they **play.***

2 Forms in the 3rd person singular

Schon bei ***have/has got*** ist die 3. Person Singular eine Sonderform. Das ist auch beim ***simple present*** so. Hier wird die Form gebildet, indem man ein ***-s*** an den Infinitiv anhängt: *he/she/it **plays.***

„He/she/it, das -s muss mit!“

Beim Anhängen des ***-s*** gelten die gleichen Regeln wie beim Plural:

- Endet das Verb mit dem Laut [ʃ] oder [ʒ], hängt man ***-es*** an: *finish – finish**es**.*
- Endet das Verb mit ***-y,*** gibt es zwei Möglichkeiten:

*Wenn vor **-y** ein Konsonant steht, wird es zu **-ie:*** *fly – fl**ies***	Wenn vor ***-y*** ein Vokal steht, bleibt es ***-y:*** *say – sa**ys***

Do und ***go*** sind in der 3. Person Singular Sonderformen: *do* – ***does,*** *go* – ***goes.***

3 Saying the 3rd person singular

Hier gelten die gleichen Regeln wie beim Plural.

- Nach stimmlosem Konsonanten, stimmlose Endung [s]: *He sits* [sɪts] *over there.*
- Nach stimmhaftem Konsonanten, stimmhafte Endung [z]: *She runs* [rʌnz] *home.*
- Nach Vokal, stimmhafte Endung [z]: *She sees* [siːz] *a dog.*
- Nach Zischlauten ([s], [z], [ʃ] oder [ʒ]) [ɪz]: *He finishes* [fɪnɪʃɪz] *his homework.*

4 Adverbs of frequency

Never, sometimes, often, usually, always *(niemals, manchmal, oft, üblicherweise, immer)* sind Häufigkeitsadverbien. Sie zeigen, dass etwas regelmäßig geschieht und tauchen oft in Sätzen auf, die im ***simple present*** stehen.

- Sie stehen normalerweise zwischen Subjekt und einfachem Verb: *I **often** sing.*
- Wenn das Verb aus mehreren Wörtern besteht (z. B. ***have got*** oder Kombinationen mit ***can/must***), steht das Adverb nach dem ersten Teil: *You can **always** call me.*
- Sie stehen nach den Formen von ***be:*** *It is **usually** sunny in summer.*

EXERCISE 1 What are the right forms?

to start:	we *start*	to rain:	it ______
to laugh:	he ______	to run:	I ______
to write:	you ______	to do:	he ______
to watch:	they ______	to go:	she ______

EXERCISE 2 How do you say it? Form the 3rd person singular. Put the verb in the right list.

to begin | to buy | to chase | to come | to fetch | to finish

to get | to help | to make | to meet | to read | to watch

[s]	[z]	[ɪz]
______	______	*chases*
______	______	______
______	______	______
______	______	______

Now listen to the audio file and check your answers.

EXERCISE 3 Put the sentences into the right order.

1 sometimes / Cecily / sing / and / together / Terfel

______.

2 in the afternoon / They / often / meet / can

______.

3 likes / the guitar / to play / Steve

______.

4 usually / plays / his band / He / with

______.

5 terrible / is / The band / never

______.

6 a lot of / They / good music / always / got / have

______.

7 the band / Terfel / every Thursday / with / plays

____

Exercise 4 An interview. Cecily is talking to Steve because she is writing an article about his band for the school magazine. Here is what he says.

Steve: "I like to play in my band.
We play rock music.
My favourite song is 'Whiskey in the Jar' by Metallica.
But I love music by other bands, too.
Terfel is our new singer."

Here is what Cecily writes:

1 *Steve likes to play in his band.*

2 ____

3 ____

4 ____

5 ____

Exercise 5 Every day ... Find the verb in the box and put in the right form.

to ask	to be	to do	to eat	to get up (2x)	to go (2x)		
to have (2x)	to make	to meet	to play	to ride	to take	to walk	

Cecily and Steve *get up* early every morning and they ______________ breakfast at home. But then their days ______________ different: Cecily ______________ the bus to school, but Steve ______________ his bike. Terfel always ______________ a little later because his house isn't far from the school. He ______________ some cornflakes for breakfast and after that he ______________ to school. The three pupils usually ______________ in the school playground and they ______________ into the classroom together. When they ______________ lunch, they ______________ plans for the afternoon. They often ______________ their homework and then they ______________ in the park. But on Thursdays, Terfel ______________ to Steve's band. He sings for them and Steve plays the guitar. Cecily ______________ a good singer, too, so Steve and the band ______________ her to sing for them with Terfel!

Exercise 1

to start:	we start	to rain:	it rains
to laugh:	he laughs	to run:	I run
to write:	you write	to do:	he does
to watch:	they watch	to go:	she goes

Exercise 2

to begin | to buy | to chase | to come | to fetch | to finish

to get | to help | to make | to meet | to read | to watch

[s]	[z]	[ɪz]
gets	begins	chases
helps	buys	fetches
makes	comes	finishes
meets	reads	watches

Exercise 3

1 sometimes / Cecily / sing / and / together / Terfel
Cecily and Terfel sometimes sing together.

2 in the afternoon / They / often / meet / can
They can often meet in the afternoon.

3 likes / the guitar / to play / Steve
Steve likes to play the guitar.

4 usually / plays / his band / He / with
He usually plays with his band.

5 terrible / is / The band / never
The band is never terrible.

6 a lot of / They / good music / always / got / have.
They have always got a lot of good music.

7 the band / Terfel / every Thursday / with / plays.
Terfel plays with the band every Thursday.

Exercise 4

Steve: "I like to play in my band.
We play rock music.
My favourite song is 'Whiskey in the Jar' by Metallica.
But I love music by other bands, too.
Terfel is our new singer."

Here is what Cecily writes:

1 Steve likes to play in his band.
2 They play rock music.
3 His favourite song is 'Whiskey in the Jar' by Metallica.
4 But he loves music by other bands, too.
5 Terfel is their newsinger./ There is a new singer in their band: it's Terfel.

Exercise 5

to ask | to be | to do | to eat | to get up (2x) | to go (2x)

to have (2x) | to make | to meet | to play | to ride | to take

to walk

Cecily and Steve **get up** early every morning and they **have** breakfast at home. But then their days are different: Cecily **takes** the bus to school, but Steve **rides** his bike. Terfel always **gets up** a little later because his house isn't far from the school. He **eats** some cornflakes for breakfast and after that he **walks** to school. The three pupils usually **meet** in the school playground and they **go** into the classroom together. When they **have** lunch, they **make** plans for the afternoon. They often **do** their homework and then they **play** in the park. But on Thursdays, Terfel **goes** to Steve's band. He sings for them and Steve plays the guitar. Cecily **is** a good singer, too, so Steve and the band **ask** her to sing for them with Terfel!

25 The simple present in negatives and questions with *to do* (Das einfache Präsens in Verneinungen und Fragen mit *to do*)

Um eine Aussage zu verneinen oder eine Frage zu bilden, braucht man im ***simple present*** *(einfaches Präsens)* das ***auxiliary*** *(Hilfsverb)* **to do** oder eine seiner gebeugten Formen.

1 Negative statements with *to do*

Es gibt im Englischen nur zwei Verben im ***simple present,*** die eigenständig eine verneinte Form bilden können:

- ***to be (am not/aren't/isn't)***
- ***have got (haven't got/hasn't got)***

Alle anderen Verben können das nicht. Sie brauchen zur Unterstützung des Hilfsverb ***to do.*** Bis auf die 3. Person Singular wird die Verneinung mit dem Hilfsverb ***don't*** + Infinitiv des ***main verb*** *(Vollverb)* gebildet:

- *I / you / we / they* ***don't watch*** *TV all day.*

Die 3. Person Singular setzt ***doesn't*** + Infinitiv des Vollverbs ein:

- *He / she / it* ***doesn't eat*** *grass.*

Wenn man ein ***adverb of frequency*** *(Häufigkeitsadverb)* benutzen will, muss man es *nach* ***don't/doesn't*** und *vor* dem Vollverb einbauen, da man nun eine mehrteilige Verbform hat:

- *Steve* ***doesn't always play*** *the guitar, he* ***sometimes plays*** *football.*

2 Questions with *to do*

Wenn man eine Frage im ***simple present*** bilden will, braucht man ***do*** bzw. ***does*** als ***auxiliary*** *(Hilfsverb).* Die Satzstellung ist dabei klar geregelt.
Bei Fragen mit einem Fragewort gilt:

question word	do/does (auxiliary)	subject	main verb	(object)	(place)	(time)
When	***does***	*Cecily*	***eat***	*lunch*	*at her house*	*on Sunday?*

Die drei Elemente in Klammern am Satzende müssen nicht bzw. nicht vollständig vorhanden sein.

Bei ***yes / no questions*** *(Entscheidungsfragen)* gilt:

do/does	subject	main verb	(object)	(place)	(time)
Do	*you*	***eat***	*lunch*	*at her house*	*on Sunday?*

- Egal, ob es ein Fragewort gibt oder nicht, die Satzstellung bleibt genau gleich.
- Nach dem Hilfsverb folgt die Standard-Satzstellung im Englischen:
  S - V - (O - Ort - Zeit).

Exercise 1 It isn't so! Turn these sentences into negative statements.

1	I like lots of homework.	I *don't like* ______ lots of homework.
2	Steve plays the piano.	Steve __________ the piano.
3	We sing a song.	We __________ a song.
4	You do your homework.	You __________ your homework.
5	It rains every Saturday.	It __________ every Saturday.
6	They eat stones.	They __________ stones.
7	You always sleep.	You __________ .
8	She often sees friends.	She __________ friends.

Exercise 2 Put these questions in the right order.

1 eat / for breakfast / does / what / Terfel

______________________________?

2 you / do / how / a birthday cake / make

______________________________?

3 Cecily / does / her friends / meet / when

______________________________?

4 does / the guitar / Steve / play / How often

______________________________?

5 want / you / to learn / English / why / do

______________________________?

Exercise 3 Make the questions and put in **do / does.**

1 rain / here / how often / it

______________________________?

2 they / do / in the afternoon / what / often

______________________________?

3 where / meet /his friends / Steve

______________________________?

4 you / orange juice / when / drink

______________________________?

Exercise 4 What **do** and **don't** they do?

Who?	No:	Yes:
1 Steve	speak French	speak English
2 Cecily and Terfel	live in Germany	live in England
3 Steve's band	play pop	play rock
4 The pupils	lie in beds	sit on chairs
5 Terfel's parents	look silly	look good
6 Cecily	play hockey	play football
7 Miss Takes	eat pizza for breakfast	eat muesli

1 Steve *doesn't speak French, he speaks English.* ______

2 Cecily and Terfel ______.

3 Steve's band ______.

4 The pupils ______.

5 Terfel's parents ______.

6 Cecily ______.

7 Miss Takes ______.

Exercise 5 Complete Terfel's e-mail and fill in the right forms.

Dear Uncle Draco, How are you? I ______ (to feel) sad that you ______ ______ (not to have) time to visit us next week. Let me tell you about my life here. I ______ (to like) my two new friends, Cecily and Steve. They aren't dragons, but they are very nice people. They ______ (to play) football and they ______ (to love) music. That's great! Cecily ______ (to sing) songs with me, but she ______ (not to play) an instrument. Steve ______ (not to sing), but he ______ (to play) the guitar. I am in his band now! I ______ (not to play) an instrument there, but I ______ (to sing) for them. Cecily ______ (not to live) in a very big house, but her house is next to a park. That's brilliant! First we ______ (to finish) our homework, then all of us ______ (to play) football there. When you ______ (to come) next time, you can go there with us. We ______ (not to want) to wait too long! Love, Terfel

Exercise 1

1 I like lots of homework.	I **don't like** lots of homework!
2 Steve plays the piano.	Steve **doesn't play** the piano!
3 We sing a song.	We **don't sing** a song!
4 You do your homework.	You **don't do** your homework!
5 It rains every Saturday.	It **doesn't rain** every Saturday!
6 They eat stones.	They **don't eat** stones!
7 You always sleep.	You **don't always sleep!**
8 She often sees friends.	She **doesn't often see** friends!

Wenn du einen vorgegebenen Satz verneinst, ist es einfach herauszufinden, ob du **do** oder **does** brauchst: Wenn das Hauptverb im bejahten Satz hinten ein **-s** hat, nimmst du **does.**
Bei den letzten beiden Sätzen gibt es Häufigkeitsadverbien, die hinter dem Hilfsverb eingebaut werden.)

Exercise 2

1 **What does Terfel eat for breakfast?**
2 **How do you make a birthday cake?**
3 **When does Cecily meet her friends?**
4 **How often does Steve play the guitar?**
5 **Why do you want to learn English?**

Exercise 3

1 **How often does it rain here?**
2 **What do they often do in the afternoon?**
3 **Where does Steve meet his friends?**
4 **When do you drink orange juice?**

Exercise 4

Who?	No:	Yes:
1 Steve	speak French	speak English
2 Cecily and Terfel	live in Germany	live in England
3 Steve's band	play pop	play rock
4 The pupils	lie in beds	sit on chairs
5 Terfel's parents	look silly	look good
7 Cecily	play hockey	play football
8 Miss Takes	eat pizza for breakfast	eat muesli

1. Steve **doesn't speak** French, he **speaks** English.
2. Cecily and Terfel **don't live** in Germany, they **live** in England.
3. Steve's band **doesn't play** pop, it **plays** rock.
4. The pupils **don't lie** in beds, they **sit** on chairs.
5. Terfel's parents **don't look** silly, they **look** good.
6. Cecily **doesn't play** hockey, she **plays** football.
7. Miss Takes **doesn't eat** pizza for breakfast, she **eats** muesli.

Exercise 5

Dear Uncle Draco, How are you? I **feel** sad that you **don't have** time to visit us next week. Let me tell you about my life here. I **like** my two new friends, Cecily and Steve.
They aren't dragons, but they are very nice people. They **play** football and they **love** music. That's great! Cecily **sings** songs with me, but she **doesn't play** an instrument. Steve **doesn't sing,** but he **plays** the guitar. I am in his band now! I **don't play** an instrument there, but I **sing** for them.
Cecily **doesn't live** in a very big house, but her house is next to a park. That's brilliant! First we **finish** our homework, then all of us **play** football there. When you **come** next time, you can go there with us. We **don't want** to wait too long!

Love, Terfel

ANSWER KEY ANSWER KEY ANSWER KEY

26 How to use the simple present and present progressive (Gegenüberstellung der einfachen und der Verlaufsform des Präsens)

1 Form

simple present	present progressive
Verb (+ 3. Person Singular ***-s***)	Form von ***to be*** + Infinitiv des Verbs + ***-ing***
*Rita **plays** the piano.*	*Rita **is playing** the piano.*
*Rita and Sissy **play** the piano.*	*Rita and Sissy **are playing** the piano.*

2 Use

simple present

Mit dem ***simple present*** drückt man aus,

- dass etwas regelmäßig / wiederholt passiert:
  ***On Mondays,** Rita **rides** her bike to Sissy's place.*
  *They **usually play** cards.*
  Signalwörter: ***always, usually normally, often, sometimes, every day, on xx days, once a month***
- dass etwas nie passiert:
  *Sissy **never goes** to Rita's place.*
  *Rita and Sissy **never play** tennis.*
  Signalwort: ***never***
- dass einzelne Handlungen nacheinander passieren:
  ***First** Rita **rides** her bike to Sissy's place.*
  ***Then,** Rita and Sissy **play** cards.*
  Signalwörter: ***first, second, after that, then, suddenly***

present progressive

Mit dem ***present progressive*** drückt man aus,

- dass etwas gerade geschieht und noch nicht vorbei ist:
  ***Look,** Rita **is riding** her bike to Sissy's place.*
  ***Now** Rita and Sissy **are playing** cards.*
  Signalwörter: ***now, this morning, at the moment, today, look***

Beachte die feinen Unterschiede bei Deutsch-Englisch-Übersetzungen:

Rita **spielt** Klavier.

simple present	present progressive
*Rita **plays** the piano.*	*Rita **is playing** the piano.*
Rita **spielt** Klavier (= kann Klavier spielen)	Rita **spielt** (= gerade im Moment) Klavier.

Exercise 1 Look at the timetable and say what Rita does every week.

Monday	to water the flowers	Friday	to bake a cake
Tuesday	to go to the cinema	Saturday	to sleep in
Wednesday	to clean the living room	Sunday	to go to church
Thursday	to wash the clothes		

1 Every Monday Rita *waters* ______________ the flowers.

2 Every Tuesday Rita ______________________________.

3 ____.

4 ____.

5 ____.

6 ____.

7 ____.

Exercise 2 Look at the pictures, compare them to the timetable in **exercise 1** and find out what day it is.

In picture 1 Rita *is cleaning the living room* ______, so it must be *Wednesday*.

In picture 2 Rita ______________________________,

so it must be ______________________________.

In picture 3 Rita ______________________________,

so it must be ______________________________.

In picture 4 Rita ______________________________,

so it must be ______________________________.

In picture 5 Rita ____.

so it must be ____.

Exercise 3 Underline the correct form.

1 Rita always <u>*goes*</u> / *is going* to the gym on Mondays.
2 Look, Rita *fights* / *is fighting* with her best friend, Sissy.
3 Rita and Sissy never *tell* / *are telling* boys their secrets *(= Geheimnisse).*
4 First Rita *takes* / *is taking* the bus to the city centre. Then she *meets* / *is meeting* her friend Sissy there. After that they *go* / *are going* into a shop. Look they *shop* / *are shopping* for clothes right now.

Exercise 4 This day is different. Write down what Rita and Sissy usually do and what they are doing today.

1 Rita usually <u>*sets*</u> the table, but today she <u>*is setting*</u> her mum's alarm clock. (to set)

2 Normally Rita and Sissy ____________________ the radio, but today they ____________________ a CD. (to listen to)

3 Rita: "Once a month I ____________________ my Dad's car, but at the moment I ____________________ the dog." (to wash)

4 Rita: "Sissy, you usually ____________________ trousers, sneakers and a T-shirt but now you ____________________ a beautiful dress. What's going on?" (to wear)

Exercise 5 Who is it? Complete the text with the simple present or present progressive.

Today Rita and Sissy ______________ (to sit) in a café and they ______________ (to play) games: Right now Sissy ____________________ (to guess) names.

Rita: "He ______________ (to be) a very famous and handsome *(= gutaussehend)* actor. Very often, he ______________ (to act) in movies with George Clooney. He and his wife Angelina never ______________ (to go out) without their children. Who ______________ (to be) it?"

Sissy: "I ______________ (to know) his name. You ______________ (to look for) ____________________!"

Exercise 1

Monday	to water the flowers	Friday	to bake a cake
Tuesday	to go to the cinema	Saturday	to sleep in
Wednesday	to clean the living room	Sunday	to go to church
Thursday	to wash the clothes		

1 Every Monday Rita **waters** the flowers.
2 Every Tuesday Rita **goes** to the cinema.
3 Every Wednesday Rita **cleans** the living room.
4 Every Thursday Rita **washes** the clothes.
5 Every Friday Rita **bakes** a cake.
6 Every Saturday Rita **sleeps in.**
7 Every Sunday Rita **goes** to church.

Exercise 2

In picture 1 Rita **is cleaning the living room,** so it must be **Wednesday.**
In picture 2 Rita **is baking a cake,** so it must be **Friday.**
In picture 3 Rita **is sleeping in,** so it must be **Saturday.**
In picture 4 Rita **is watering the flowers,** so it must be **Monday.**
In picture 5 Rita **is washing the clothes,** so it must be **Thursday.**

Exercise 3

1 Rita always **goes** / **is going** to the gym on Mondays.
2 Look, Rita **fights** / **is fighting** with her best friend.
3 Rita and Sissy never **tell** / **are telling** boys their secrets (= Geheimnisse).
4 First Rita **takes** / **is taking** the bus to the city centre. Then she **meets** / **is meeting** her friend Sissy there. After that they **go** / **are going** into a shop. Look they **shop** / **are shopping** for clothes right now.

Exercise 4

1 Rita usually **sets** the table, but today she **is setting** her mum's alarm clock.
2 Normally Rita and Sissy **listen to** the radio, but today they **are listening to** a CD.
3 Rita: "Once a month I **wash** my Dad's car, but at the moment I **am washing** the dog."
4 Rita: "Sissy, you usually **wear** trousers, sneakers and a T-shirt, but now you **are wearing** a beautiful dress. What's going on?"

Exercise 5

Today Rita and Sissy **are sitting** in a café and they **are playing** games: Right now Sissy **is guessing** names.

Rita: "He **is** a very famous and handsome (= gutaussehend) actor. Very often he **acts** in movies with George Clooney. He and his wife Angelina never **go out** without their children.
Who **is** it?"

Sissy: "I **know** his name. You **are looking for Brad Pitt!**"

ANSWER KEY ANSWER KEY ANSWER KEY

The present progressive

EXERCISE 1 A fight for the bathroom. Complete the dialogue.

Matt and his dad ____________________ (to wait) in front of the bathroom in the morning. Matt's sister Joeleen ____________________ (to sing) in the bathroom.

Matt: "What ____________________ (you / to do) in there?"

Joeleen: "I ____________________ (to take) a shower! ____________________ (I / to sing) well?"

Dad: "No, you ____________________ (short answer). ____________________ (you / to wash) your hair, too?"

Joeleen: "Yes, I ____________________ (short answer). Just five more minutes!"

Dad and Matt: "Hurry up!!!"

8 P

EXERCISE 2 Look at the picture and write down what is happening.

Taylor and Kim – Ben The dog – Henry The two old ladies	is – are	laughing – sitting on the grass reading a book – playing football sleeping under a tree

1 ______________________________

2 ______________________________

3 ______________________________

4 ______________________________

5 ______________________________

5 P

EXERCISE 3 Look at the picture again! Then tick the correct box and write down what these people are doing and what they aren't doing.

1	Marie	☐	sing a song	listen to her iPod	☐
2	Dennis	☐	fish	play the guitar	☐
3	Jen and Nan	☐	look at a magazine	fight	☐
4	A man	☐	wait for somebody	feed the birds	☐
5	Two babies	☐	cry	drink milk	☐

1 ______________________________
____

2 ______________________________
____

3 ______________________________
____

4 ______________________________
____

5 ______________________________
____
____

15 P

The simple present

EXERCISE 4 Austin's Facebook friends. Use the **simple present** to complete their profiles.

Julie

Julie ____________ (to come) from Dallas, TX. Austin ____________ (to know) her because she ____________ (to be) an exchange student at his school. Julie ____________ (to like) basketball and ____________ (have got) a poster of Dirk Nowitzki in her room. She ____________ (not to play) basketball, but she ____________ (to run) every morning because she ____________ (to want) to stay fit.

Mark

Mark ____________ (not to be) Austin's brother, but they ____________ (to look) alike *(= ähneln sich)*. Mark and Austin ____________ (to be) in the same Boy Scout troop, but they ____________ (not to go) to the same school. Mark ____________ (to go) to Taylor Hills High School, Austin to Woodridge Middle School. Mark's mum always ____________ (to worry) about his marks because he ____________ (to spend) a lot of time with the Boy Scouts.

Susi and Maike

Susi and Maike ____________ (to be) Austin's cousins from Germany. Susi ____________(to love) photography and usually ____________ (to carry) her camera around. Austin and Susi ____________ (to write) a lot of e-mails, but he ____________ (not to phone) her very often. Maike ____________ (to be) interested in cooking and ____________ (to hope) to be a chef one day! Austin ____________ (to enjoy) her desserts very much when he ____________ (to visit) her in Germany.

12 P

EXERCISE 5 Ask questions and give answers. You will find the facts in the profiles of Austin's Facebook friends. Sometimes you only need **short answers.**

1 **Julie**

Julie / to come / Texas?

____

to know / How / Austin / her ?

____

2 **Mark**

Mark and Austin / brothers / to be?

____

Who / a lot of time / Mark / to spend / with?

____

3 **Susi and Maike**

Where / from / to be / they?

____

Austin / to enjoy / Maike's desserts?

____

12 P

EXERCISE 6 Signal words. Translate these signal words for the **simple present** and put them in the crossword puzzle. Then use them to write about a typical afternoon in your family (50–60 words).

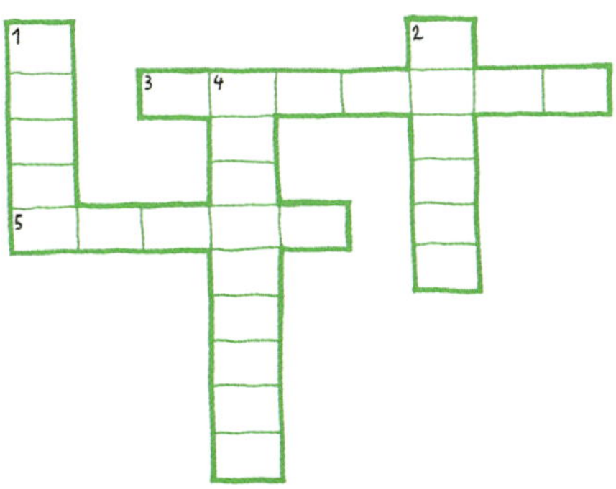

Across
3. normalerweise
5. nie

Down
1. oft
2. immer
4. manchmal

____

15 P

Simple present or present progressive?

EXERCISE 7 What is different today? Fill in the missing words. Use the **simple present** or the **present progressive form.**

Matt always ____________ (to sleep) until 9.30 am on Saturday. But today he ____________ (to be) up early. At 7 am he ____________ (to get) ready for a fishing trip. Usually, Matt ____________ (to do) his homework on Saturday morning, but now he ____________ (to look for) his boots. He ____________ (not to know) where they ____________ (to be). His dad ____________ (to call) from the car.

Dad: "Hurry! I ____________ (not to want) to be late! We never ____________ (to catch) anything after 9 am. ____________ (to be) you ready?"

Matt: "I ____________ (to come)! Mum, what ________ ________ (you/to do)?"

Mum: "I ____________ (to take) out the pans *(= Bratpfannen)* for the fish. ____________ (to have) fun!"

13 P

EXERCISE 8 A day in the garden. First listen. Then write down what the people are doing. Finally describe the day.

Mr Bogle: ____.

Mrs Bogle: ____.

Sarah: ____.

Austin: ____.

Austin's friends: ____.

Grandma: ____.

6 P

Describe the day: ____.

____

____

4 P

Auswertung Trage rechts deine Gesamtpunktzahl ein und vergleiche.

☺ 90 – 69 points	😐 68 – 46 points	☹ 45 – 0 points

TOTAL SCORE 90 P

Exercise 1
are waiting | is singing | are you doing | am taking | Aren't I singing/Am I singing | aren't | Are you washing | am

Exercise 2
1 Taylor and Kim are playing football.
2 Ben is reading a book.
3 The dog is sleeping under the tree.
4 Henry is sitting on the grass.
5 The two old ladies are laughing.

Exercise 3
1	Marie		sing a song	listen to her iPod	✗
2	Dennis	✗	fish	play the guitar	
3	Jen and Nan		look at a magazine	fight	✗
4	A man	✗	wait for somebody	feed the birds	
5	Two babies	✗	cry	drink milk	

Marie is listening to her iPod. She isn't singing a song.
Dennis is fishing. He isn't playing the guitar.
Jen and Nan are fighting. They aren't looking at a magazine.
A man is waiting for somebody. He isn't feeding the birds.
Two babies are crying. They aren't drinking milk.

Exercise 4
Julie: comes | knows - is | likes - has got | doesn't play - runs - wants
Mark: isn't - look | are - don't go | goes | worries - spends
Susi and Maike: are | loves - carries | write - doesn't phone | is - hopes | enjoys - visits

Exercise 5
1 **Julie:** **Does Julie come from Texas?** Yes, she does.
How does Austin know her? She is an exchange student at his school.
2 **Mark:** **Are Mark and Austin brothers?** No, they aren't.
Who does Mark spend a lot of time with? He spends a lot of time with the Boy Scouts.
3 **Susi and Maike:** **Where are they from?** They are from Germany.
Does Austin enjoy Maike's desserts? Yes, he does.

Exercise 6
Down: **1** often **2** always **4** sometimes **Across:** **3** usually **5** never
Lösungsbeispiel:
I usually come home from school at 2 pm. But I never do my homework right after lunch. First, I play with my little sister. She often wants to do a puzzle. Then, we sometimes have a snack in the afternoon before I start my homework. When Dad comes home from work, we always have dinner together.

Exercise 7
sleeps | is | is getting | does - is looking for | doesn't know - are | is calling | don't want | catch | Are | am coming | are you doing | am taking | Have

Exercise 8
Mr Bogle is cutting the bushes in front of the house.
Mrs Bogle is planting flowers next to the front door.
Sarah is watering the plants.
Austin is painting the balcony.
Austin's friends are going to the football field.
Grandma is bringing pizza for dinner.

It is a warm and sunny spring day. There are no clouds in the sky.

27 Ordinal numbers and saying the date (Ordnungszahlen und Datumsangaben)

Um eine Reihenfolge oder ein Datum anzugeben, verwendet man ***ordinal numbers*** *(Ordnungszahlen)* wie *der erste, die zweite, das dritte* usw.

1 Ordinal numbers and their forms

Die einfachen Zahlen *(Kardinalzahlen)* wie vier, sieben oder neunzehn sind dir schon bekannt. Die Ordnungszahlen werden meistens dadurch bildet, dass man an die Kardinalzahl ein ***-th*** anhängt:

*four – four**th***	*seven – seven**th***	*nineteen – nineteen**th***

Es gibt einige Ausnahmen von dieser Regel: Hier pass auf beim Sprechen und Schreiben:

*one – **first***	*two – **second***	*three – **third***
*five – **fifth***	*eight – eigh**th***	*nine – nin**th***
*twelve – twel**fth***	*twenty – twent**ieth***	*twenty-one – twenty-**first***
*thirty – thirt**ieth***	Die nachfolgenden Zehnerzahlen enden auch auf ***-ieth.***	

Die Endung der jeweiligen Ordnungszahl fügt man auch an, wenn man sie nicht als Wort, sondern als Zahl schreibt:

first – 1st/1st	*second – 2nd/2nd*	*third – 3rd/3rd*
fourth – 4th/4th	*twenty-seventh – 27th/27th*	*forty-second – 42nd/42nd*

Du kannst die Endung dabei direkt auf die Zeile oder hochgestellt schreiben.

2 Saying the date

Beim Datum gibt es einen Unterschied zwischen der Schreibweise und der Art und Weise, wie man es mündlich formuliert.

Man schreibt:	Man sagt:
6th April	***the** sixth **of** April*
23rd July	***the** twenty-third **of** July*
His birthday is on 13th October.	*His birthday is on **the** thirteenth **of** October.*
We can meet on 2nd May.	*We can meet on **the** second **of** May.*

Die Jahreszahlen werden so gelesen:

1993	*nineteen ninety-three*
2011	*two thousand and eleven oder twenty eleven*

EXERCISE 1 Change into ordinal numbers and write them down in numbers and in words.

number	ordinal number	ordinal number in words
64 →	64th	sixty-fourth
15 →		
150 →		
83 →		
77 →		
409 →		
91 →		
38 →		
52 →		

EXERCISE 2 When are their birthdays? Find out and write down how you say them.

Miss Takes
– 2nd February

Cecily
– 4th June

Mr Beemer
– 1st December

Terfel
– 9th November

Steve
– 13th January

Franz Beckenbauer
– 9th September

Sebastian Vettel
– 3rd July

My birthday
–

1 *Miss Takes' birthday is on the second of February.*

2 Cecily's birthday is ______________________.

3 ______________________.

4 ______________________.

5 ______________________.

6 ______________________.

7 ______________________.

8 My birthday is ______________________.

EXERCISE 3 This is Steve's notebook. What does he do when? How do you say it?

1 *On the sixth of January Steve is visiting his grandma in Leeds*

2 On ______________________.

3 ______________________.

4 ______________________.

5 ______________________.

6 ______________________.

EXERCISE 4 Translate these sentences into German. Which German tense do you use?

1 *Am 6. Januar besucht Steve seine Großmutter in Leeds.*

2 ______________________.

3 ______________________.

4 ______________________.

5 ______________________.

6 ______________________.

Exercise 1

number	ordinal number	ordinal number in words
64	64th	sixty-fourth
15	15th	fifteenth
150	150th	one hundred and fiftieth / a hundred and fiftieth
83	83rd	eighty-third
77	77th	seventy-seventh
409	409th	four hundred and ninth
91	91st	ninety-first
38	38th	thirty-eighth
52	52nd	fifty-second

Exercise 2

Miss Takes
2nd February

Cecily
4th June

Mr Beemer
1st December

Terfel
9th November

Steve
13th January

Franz Becken-
bauer
9th September

Sebastian Vettel
3rd July

My birthday

1 Miss Takes' birthday is on the second of February.
2 Cecily's birthday is on the fourth of June.
3 Mr Beemer's birthday is on the first of December.
4 Terfel's birthday is on the ninth of November.
5 Steve's birthday is on the thirteenth of January.
6 Franz Beckenbauer's birthday is on the ninth of September.
7 Sebastian Vettel's birthday is on the third of July.
8 My birthday is on the ??? of ???.

Exercise 3

1	On the sixth of January Steve is visiting his grandma in Leeds.
2	On the twenty-second of February he is going skiing with his family.
3	On the fifth of May he is meeting his cousin Joe in a restaurant.
4	On the fourth of June he is celebrating Cecily's birthday party.
5	On the third of August he is going to the zoo to see the penguins.
6	On the thirty-first of October he is having a Halloween party.

Bei dieser Übung verwendest du das **present progressive** (→ Modul 22). Achte auf die richtige Bildung (Form von **to be** + Verb + **ing).** Das **present progressive** drückt hier aus, dass die Ereignisse genau am genannten Tag stattfinden (werden).

Exercise 4

1 Am 6. Januar besucht Steve seine Großmutter in Leeds.
2 Am 22. Februar geht er Skifahren mit seiner Familie.
3 Am 5. Mai trifft er seinen Cousin José im Restaurant.
4 Am 4. Juni feiert er auf Cecilys Geburtstagsparty.
(Oder: Am 4. Juni feiert er Cecilys Geburtstagsparty).
5 Am 3. August geht er zum Zoo, um die Pinguine zu sehen.
6 Am 31. Oktober gibt er eine Halloween-Party.

German tense: Das einfache Präsens.

ANSWER KEY ANSWER KEY ANSWER KEY

28 Telling the time (Zeitangaben)

1 Simple time units

Die Uhrzeit anzugeben funktioniert in Englisch fast immer genauso wie in Deutsch. Folgende Begriffe braucht man:

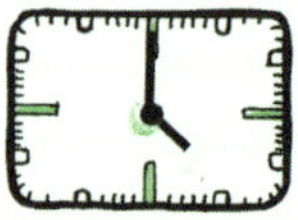

It's five o'clock.

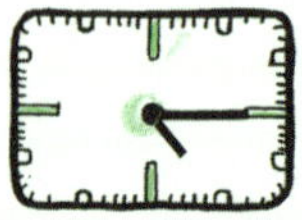

It's quarter past five.

It's ***half past*** *five.*

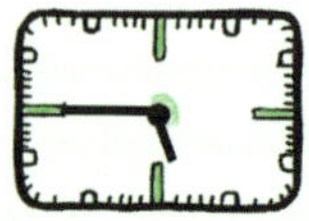

It's quarter to six.

Bei ***half past*** erkennt man den wichtigsten Unterschied zum Deutschen:
Das Englische gibt an, dass es eine halbe Stunde **nach** einer bestimmten vollen Stunde ist. Im Deutschen sagt man, dass es noch eine halbe Stunde bis **zur nächsten** vollen Stunde dauert: Es ist halb sechs. = *It's half past five.*

It's five past five.

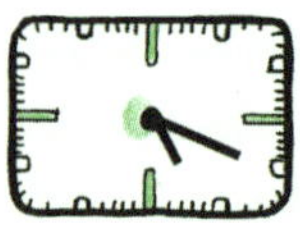

It's twenty past five.

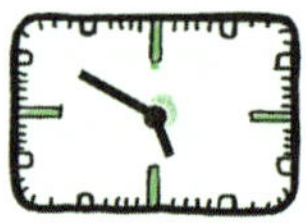

It's ten to six.

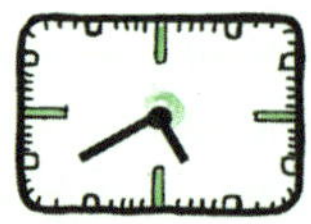

It's twenty-three ***minutes*** *to six.*

Wenn die Zeitangabe Fünfer- oder Zehnerzahlen enthält, lässt du das Wort ***minutes*** weg, bei anderen Zahlwörtern brauchst du es.

2 Digital time units

Man kann die Zeit auch wie bei einer Digitaluhr angeben, indem man einfach die Zahlenwerte liest.

It's five thirty-four.

It's five ***o*** *six.*

Hier ist darauf zu achten, dass man bei einer **Minutenzahl unter zehn** die Null der Digitaluhr als ***o*** mitliest.

3 The time of day

Englische Zeitangaben beschränken sich auf eine Einteilung in zwölf Stunden (außer bei Fahrplänen), ein Uhr nachmittags ist also nicht, wie in Deutsch, mit dreizehn Uhr zu umschreiben. Wenn es notwendig ist, die Tageszeit klarzustellen, geht das mit den Angaben ***am*** (vor zwölf Uhr mittags) und ***pm*** (nach zwölf Uhr mittags), aber **nicht** in Kombination mit ***o'clock:***

- *It's three* ***am.*** = Es ist drei Uhr **morgens.**
- *It's three* ***pm.*** = Es ist drei Uhr **nachmittags.**

Exercise 1 What's the time? Write down how you say the time.

1 *It's twelve minutes to three.*

2 It's ______.

3 ______.

4 ______.

5 ______.

6 ______.

7 ______.

8 ______.

And now?

1	9:05	*It's nine o five*
2	6:18	It's ______.
3	2:56	______.
4	4:47	______.
5	8:09	______.
6	10:34	______.
7	3:22	______.
8	7:41	______.

Exercise 2 Translate these times.

◷ = round clock	▭ = digital clock	☼ = morning	☽ = afternoon/night

1 Es ist dreizehn Uhr vier. ◷ ☽

It's four minutes past one pm.

2 Es ist neun Uhr vierundvierzig. ▭ ☼ ______________________________.

______________________________.

3 Es ist dreiundzwanzig Uhr eins. ▭ ☽ ______________________________.

______________________________.

Exercise 3 What are they doing, and when?

1 *It's quarter to eight. Cecily is getting up.*

2 It's ______________________________.

Terfel ______________________________.

3 ______________________________.

4 ______________________________.

5 ______________________________.

6 ______________________________.

7 ______________________________.

8 ______________________________.

Exercise 1

1 It's twelve minutes to three.
2 It's quarter past one.
3 It's twenty-four (twenty-three) minutes past nine.
4 It's twenty to seven.
5 It's eleven o'clock.
6 It's eleven (twelve) minutes past eight.
7 It's quarter to four.
8 it's twenty-five to five.

And now?

1 It's nine o five.
2 It's six eighteen.
3 It's two fifty-six.
4 It's four forty-seven.
5 It's eight o nine.
6 It's ten thirty-four.
7 It's three twenty-two.
8 It's seven forty-one.

Exercise 2

1 Es ist dreizehn Uhr vier. ⏱ ❍

It's four minutes past one pm.

2 Es ist neun Uhr vierundvierzig. ▭ ☼.

It's nine forty-four am.

3 Es ist dreiundzwanzig Uhr eins. ▭ ❍.

It's eleven o one pm.

Exercise 3

1 It's quarter to eight. Cecily is getting up.

2 It's ten past eight. Terfel is having breakfast./Terfel is eating cornflakes.

3 It's twenty-six minutes to nine. Steve is riding his bike to school.

4 It's ten o'clock. Cecily, Steve and Terfel are learning./Cecily, Steve and Terfel are having a lesson./Cecily, Steve and Terfel are sitting in their class.

5 It's half past three. Cecily and Steve are playing football.

6 It's twenty-five to five. Steve and Terfel are playing a computer (video) game.

„Etwas am Computer spielen" kann im Englischen nicht ohne **game** ausgedrückt werden.

7 It's five to six. Cecily and Terfel are singing (a song).

8 It's seven minutes past nine. Miss Takes is watching TV.

29 Word order in statements with adverbial phrases and adverbs of frequency (Wortstellung in Aussagesätzen mit Adverbialbestimmungen und Adverbien der Häufigkeit)

Die Wortstellung im englischen Aussagesatz ist: ***subject* - *verb* - *object* (S - V - O).**

I **(S)** *have* **(V)** *lunch* **(O).**

1 Word order in statements with adverbial phrases

Wenn der Satz neben Subjekt, Verb und Objekt zusätzlich ***adverbial phrases*** *(Adverbialbestimmungen),* z. B. **des Ortes und der Zeit** enthält, stehen diese meist am Satzende:

I **(S)** *have* **(V)** *lunch* **(O)** *at home* **(Adv Ort)** *on Sundays* **(Adv Zeit).**

Dabei gilt: Die Adverbialbestimmung des Ortes steht **vor** der Adverbialbestimmung der Zeit (wie im Alphabet: ***O**rt* vor ***Z**eit,* ebenso: ***p**lace* vor ***t**ime*). Will man die Zeitangabe inhaltlich hervorheben, kann man sie an den Satzanfang stellen.

S - V - O bleibt aber erhalten, anders als im Deutschen:

On Sundays **(Adv Zeit),** *I* **(S)** *have* **(V)** *lunch* **(O)** *at home* **(Adv Ort).**

Sonntags **(Adv Zeit)** esse **(V)** ich **(S)** zu Hause **(Adv Ort)** Mittag **(O).**

Du siehst: Verb und Objekt bilden im englischen Satz eine Einheit (S - V - O). Es darf - anders als im Deutschen - nichts zwischen den beiden stehen. Adverbialbestimmungen werden deshalb meist ans Satzende gestellt (wie im Beispiel die Modalbestimmung):

I **(S)** *like* **(V)** *apples* **(O)** *so much* **(Adv).** Ich **(S)** mag **(V)** so gerne **(Adv)** Äpfel **(O).**

2 Word order in statements with adverbs of frequency

Adverbs of frequency *(Adverbien der Häufigkeit)* geben an, wie oft man etwas tut. Als Satzglieder gehören sie zu den Adverbialbestimmungen. Es sind z. B. ***always, usually, often, sometimes*** und ***never.*** Auch diese dürfen nicht zwischen Verb und Objekt stehen und befinden sich im Englischen meist **vor** dem Verb:

I **(S)** *often* **(Adv)** *call* **(V)** *my Mum* **(O).** Ich **(S)** rufe **(V)** oft **(Adv)** meine Mama **(O)** an.

Will man sie inhaltlich besonders hervorheben, kann man ***usually*** und ***sometimes*** (und nur diese!) an den Satzanfang stellen, also (Adv - S - V - O).

*We **sometimes** watch TV.*	Wir schauen **manchmal** fern. *(normal)*
***Sometimes** we watch TV.*	**Manchmal** schauen wir fern. *(hervorgehoben)*

Ausnahmen von der Regel „Nichts zwischen Verb und Objekt usw." bilden das Verb ***to be*** und Hilfsverben. Werden diese Verben im Satz verwendet, so steht das ***adverb of frequency*** nach dem Verb ***to be*** und nach dem Hilfsverb (also vor dem Vollverb).

*Ben is **never** late for school.*

*You can **always** use my computer.*

Exercise 1 Rewrite the sentences and put the **adverb of frequency** in the right position.

1 He listens to the radio. (often)

____.

2 They watch TV in the morning. (never)

____.

3 I am hungry. (often)

____.

4 He helps his father in the garden. (usually)

____.

5 Mr Smith goes for a walk in the evening. (always)

____.

6 My teacher is very friendly. (usually)

____.

7 She takes sugar in her coffee. (sometimes)

____.

8 My mother gets angry. (never)

____.

9 She can go to the swimming pool. (always)

____.

10 Do you go to London? (often)

____.

11 I don't get up before 10 am. (usually)

____.

12 He is very sleepy in the afternoon. (always)

____.

13 She meets him at the weekend. (never)

____.

Exercise 2 Put the words together to form correct sentences.

1 I / play tennis / never / at the weekend

____.

2 swimming / They / in the lake / usually / go

____.

3 in the evening / TV / Jim / watches / sometimes

____.

4 on Saturday / They / meet / never

____.

5 coffee / does not / He / usually / drink

____.

6 tests / often / do / must / We

____.

7 spaghetti / Kids / like / usually / very much

____.

Exercise 3 Translate the sentences below.

1 Samstags gehe ich oft ins Kino.

____.

2 Sie schläft nachts nie im Garten.

____.

3 Er hilft ihr gewöhnlich gern bei ihren Hausaufgaben.

____.

4 Ich komme nie gern zu spät.

____.

5 Sie gehen nie in den Zoo.

____.

Exercise 1

1 He listens to the radio. (often)
He **often** listens to the radio.

2 They watch TV in the morning. (never)
They **never** watch TV in the morning.

3 I am hungry. (often)
I am **often** hungry.

4 He helps his father in the garden. (usually)
He **usually** helps his father in the garden.

5 Mr Smith goes for a walk in the evening. (always)
Mr Smith **always** goes for a walk in the evening.

6 My teacher is very friendly. (usually)
My teacher is **usually** very friendly.

7 She takes sugar in her coffee. (sometimes)
She **sometimes / Sometimes** she takes sugar in her coffee.

8 My mother gets angry. (never)
My mother **never** gets angry.

9 She can go to the swimming pool. (always)
She can **always** go to the swimming pool.

10 Do you go to London? (often)
Do you **often** go to London?

11 I don't get up before 10 am. (usually)
I don't **usually / Usually** I don't get up before 10 am.

12 He is very sleepy in the afternoon. (always)
He is **always** very sleepy in the afternoon.

13 She meets him at the weekend. (never)
She **never** meets him at the weekend.

Exercise 2

1 I / play / tennis / never / at the weekend
I never play tennis at the weekend.

2 swimming / They / in the lake / usually / go
They usually go swimming in the lake.

3 in the evening / TV / Jim / watches / sometimes
Jim sometimes watches TV in the evening.

4 on Saturday / They / meet / never
They never meet on Saturday.

5 coffee / does not / He / usually / drink
He does not usually drink coffee.

6 tests / often / do / must / We
We must often do tests.

7 spaghetti / Kids / like / usually / very much
Kids usually like spaghetti very much.

Exercise 3 ☆

1 Samstags gehe ich oft ins Kino.
I often go to the cinema on Saturdays. / (betont:)
On Saturdays I often go to the cinema.

2 Sie schläft nachts nie im Garten.
She never sleeps in the garden at night.

3 Er hilft ihr gewöhnlich gern bei ihren Hausaufgaben.
He usually likes to help her with her homework. /
(betont:) **Usually he likes to help her with her homework.**

4 Ich komme nie gern zu spät.
I never like to be late.

5 Sie gehen nie in den Zoo.
They never go to the zoo.

30 Questions with question words and the verb *to do* (Fragewort-Fragen mit dem Hilfsverb *to do*)

Für die Bildung der Fragewort-Frage wird im Englischen meist ein ***auxiliary*** *(Hilfsverb)*, z. B. ***to be*** oder ***can,*** verwendet:

- *What **can** we buy for Austin's birthday? (We **can** buy a DVD.)*

Wenn jedoch kein Hilfsverb im Aussagesatz vorhanden ist, muss ***do / does*** nach dem Fragewort in der Frage eingefügt werden.

- *Where **do** you go after school? (I go to Grandma's house.)*

Bei der 3. Person Singular wird ***does*** verwendet, bei den übrigen Personen ***do.***
Das ***main verb*** *(Vollverb,* hier ***go****)* steht jeweils im Infinitiv.

1 Word order in questions with question words and *to do*

Die Wortstellung in Fragewort-Fragen mit ***do/does*** entspricht der Wortstellung in den Entscheidungsfragen. Das Fragewort wird vorangestellt.

question word	auxiliary	subject	main verb	object
What	**do**	*you*	*eat*	*at Thanksgiving?*
Where	**does**	*Ryan*	*work?*	
When	**do**	*they*	*go*	*to bed?*
How	**does**	*she*	*like*	*Dublin?*
How often	**do**	*you*	*play*	*football?*
Why	**do**	*we*	*visit*	*Uncle Jim every Sunday?*

Auch die verneinte Frage ist gebräuchlich:

*What **don't** you like about it?*	Was gefällt dir daran nicht?

Bei der verneinten Frage mit ***Why don't …?*** handelt es sich oft um einen Vorschlag:

***Why don't** we play football?* ***Why do** we **not** play football?*	Wieso spielen wir nicht Fußball?

Das Verb ***to do*** kommt zweimal im Fragesatz vor, wenn es Hilfsverb und Vollverb ist.

*What **do** you **do** after dinner? (I usually play with my sister.)*

2 Exception: *Who* and *What* as subject

Eine Ausnahme bildet die Frage nach dem Subjekt eines Satzes mit ***Who?*** oder ***What?*** Dabei wird kein Hilfsverb verwendet:

- ***Who** visits Uncle Jim every Sunday? (We visit Uncle Jim every Sunday.)*
- ***What** is in your bag? (There are two books in my bag.)*

In Modul 31 findest du zur Frage nach dem Subjekt eines Satzes mehr Informationen.

Exercise 1 **Do** or **does?**

1 When ____________ you usually start football practice?

2 Why ____________ Coach Brown wear this funny hat all the time?

3 What ____________ we need to take to football practice?

4 How ____________ the other team play?

5 Where ____________ he put the balls after football practice?

Exercise 2 Lots of questions. Matt is the new boy in Austin's Boy Scout troop. He is talking to him for the first time. Form questions with **do** or **does.**

Austin: "Hi Matt! How ____________ (you / to like) it here?"

Matt: "It's wonderful. I like the town and the new school. But where ____________ (you / to go) for dinner here? There are no restaurants!"

Austin: "I know. It's a small town. What ____________ (your sister / to think) about the new pet shop? I know she has got a rabbit."

Matt: "Well, she is very excited. When ____________ (it / to open) in the morning?"

Austin: "I think it opens at 9 am. Why ____________ (we / not to go) together on Saturday?"

Matt: "Great! See you then."

Exercise 3 Ask for the underlined parts of the sentences.

1 I always get up <u>at 6 am.</u>

____________?

2 We go <u>to Florida</u> every summer.

____________?

3 My sister likes <u>dolphins.</u>

____________?

4 Mr Ellis goes <u>to a Manchester United football match every Saturday.</u>

____________?

5 Because a glass of milk in the morning is healthy.

____?

7 Because I don't know how to play chess.

____?

8 I brush my teeth after I get up.

____?

Exercise 4 Matt has more and more questions. Write down five possible sensible *(= sinnvolle)* questions with the sentence parts below.

When	do / does	I	do on Sundays?
Where		you	wear school uniforms?
What		he / she / it	leave for church?
How long		we	stay in Florida?
Why		they	meet the other Boy Scouts?

1 ____?

2 ____?

3 ____?

4 ____?

5 ____?

Exercise 5 Form the correct question.

1 What / say / your Mum / does

____?

2 do / like / How / you / my new shirt

____?

3 Why / you / out of the window / do / look / in Ms Jackson's class

____?

4 with their dog / go for a walk / do / they / When

____?

Exercise 1

1	When	**do**	you usually start football practice?
2	Why	**does**	Coach Brown wear this funny hat all the time?
3	What	**do**	we need to take to football practice?
4	How	**does**	the other team play?
5	Where	**does**	he put the balls after football practice?

Exercise 2

Austin: "Hi Matt! How **do you like** it here?"

Matt: "It's wonderful. I like the town and the new school. But where **do you go** for dinner here? There are no restaurants!"

Austin: "I know. It's a small town. What **does your sister think** about the new pet shop?
I know she has got a rabbit."

Matt: "Well, she is very excited. When **does it open** in the morning?"

Austin: "I think it opens at 9 am. Why **don't we go/do we not go** together on Saturday?"

Matt: "Great! See you then."

Exercise 3

1	When do you get up?	I always get up at 6 am.
2	Where do you go every summer?	We go to Florida every summer.
3	What does your sister like?	My sister likes dolphins.
4	Where does Mr Ellis go every Saturday?	Mr Ellis goes to a Manchester United football match every Saturday.
5	Why do you (always) drink a glass of milk in the morning?	Because a glass of milk in the morning is healthy.
6	Why don't you play chess?	Because I don't know how to play chess.
7	What do you do after you get up?	I brush my teeth after I get up.

Exercise 4

When do I / you / we / they leave for church?
When does he / she leave for church?
When do I / you / we / they meet the other Boy Scouts?
When does he / she meet the other Boy Scouts?

Where do I / you / we / they stay in Florida?
Where does he / she stay in Florida?
Where do I / you / we / they meet the other Boy Scouts?
Where does he / she meet the other Boy Scouts?

What do I / you / we / they do on Sundays?
What does he / she do on Sundays?

How long do I / you / we / they stay in Florida?
How long does he / she stay in Florida?

Why do you I / you / we / they wear school uniforms?
Why does he / she wear school uniforms?
Why do I / you / we / they leave for church?
Why does he / she leave for church?
Why do I / you / we / they stay in Florida?
Why does he / she stay in Florida?
Why do I / you / we / they meet the other Boy Scouts?
Why does he / she meet the other Boy Scouts?

Exercise 5

1 What / say / your Mum / does?
What does your Mum say?

2 do / like / How / you / my new shirt?
How do you like my new shirt?

3 Why / you / out of the window / do / look / in Ms Jackson's class?
Why do you look out of the window in Ms Jackson's class?

4 with their dog / go for a walk / do / they / When?
When do they go for a walk with their dog?

ANSWER KEY ANSWER KEY ANSWER KEY

31 Questions with question words and *to be, have got, must, can* (Fragewort-Fragen mit *to be, have got, must, can*)

Für die Bildung von Fragewort-Fragen im Englischen wird meist das ***auxiliary*** *(Hilfsverb)* ***do/does*** verwendet. (→ Modul 30). Man kann auch Fragewort-Fragen mit den ***auxiliaries can, must*** oder ***have got*** bilden:

- *Where **can** we go to get Austin's present? – We **can** go to Harrods.*
- *What **have** you **got** in your bag? – I **have got** two new shirts in my bag.*

To be kann ***main verb*** *(Vollverb)* der Fragewort-Frage oder ***auxiliary*** sein, wie z. B. im ***present progressive.***

1 *Must, can* and *have got* in questions with question words

In Fragewort-Fragen mit ***can*** und ***must*** ist die Wortstellung dieselbe wie in den Entscheidungsfragen bzw. den Fragewort-Fragen mit ***do/does.*** Das Fragewort wird vor das Hilfsverb gestellt, es folgen das Subjekt, Vollverb und Objekt/Adverbialbestimmung.

question word	auxiliary	subject	main verb	object/adverbial phrase
What	**can**	*you*	*eat*	*at the pub?*
Where	**must**	*she*	*go?*	
When	**can**	*they*	*come*	*to London?*
How	**can**	*I*	*do*	*this exercise?*

Die Fragewort-Frage mit ***have got*** folgt diesem Beispiel ebenfalls.

- *What **have** you **got** in your bag?*

Can und ***must*** sind für alle Personen unveränderlich. ***Have got*** wird jedoch in der 3. Person Singular zu ***has got.*** Die Verneinung ***can't*** bedeutet *nicht können,* aber ***mustn't*** heißt übersetzt *nicht dürfen.*

- *Why **can't** Richard come at the weekend?*

2 *To be* as main verb and auxiliary in questions with question words

Ist ***to be*** das ***main verb*** der Fragesatz-Frage, wird kein ***auxiliary*** bei der Fragebildung verwendet. Wie im Deutschen folgt auf das Fragewort die Form von ***to be:***

- *Where **are** you?* – Wo bist du?
- *What **is** in your suitcase?* – Was ist in deinem Koffer?
- *How long **is** this film?* – Wie lang ist dieser Film?

Ist ***to be*** jedoch ***auxiliary*** *(Hilfsverb),* wie z. B. im ***present progressive,*** entspricht die Wortstellung der mit anderen Hilfsverben.

question word	auxiliary	subject	main verb	object/adverbial phrase
Where	**is**	*he*	*eating*	*his lunch?*
What	**are**	*you*	*reading?*	
Why	**is**	*Sandra*	*writing*	*a letter?*

EXERCISE 1 Carlos, the magician, is at Woodridge Middle School today. During his performance, the children have a lot of questions for him.

a) Write down their questions. Find the right auxiliary (if necessary).

1 Which trick / now / do / you

____?

2 not show / us / Why / you / the cards

____?

3 can / you / do / with your hat / What

____?

4 behind your back / What / have got / you

____?

5 Why / a pink bow / the bunny / has got

____?

b) Add the correct question words to the following questions.

____________________ haven't you got another card trick?

____________________ can you come back? Next week perhaps?

____________________ can the bunny jump? Two metres?

____________________ is the magician? I can't see him.

c) Elyse is always worried. She wants answers to the following questions. Complete her questions with **must** or **can.**

Where ____________________ we go after the performance?

When ____________________ I get the magician's autograph?

When ____________________ we be back in our classrooms?

Where ____________________ the bunny be?

d) Before the performance, the magician had some questions for the principal of Woodridge Middle School. Translate his questions.

1 Wo kann ich meinen Hut ablegen?

____?

2 Wann muss ich fertig sein?

____?

3 Wieso kann ich diesen Tisch nicht benutzen?

____?

4 Wie lang sind die Unterrichtsstunden?

____?

e) The principal, Mr King, had a few questions for the magician, too. Write down his questions.

1 Den Direktor interessiert, wie viele Kinder dem Zauberer zuschauen können.

How many children can watch you?

2 Er möchte wissen, was der Hase gerade im Hut des Zauberers macht.

____?

3 Er fragt, was in dem großen Korb des Zauberers ist.

____?

4 Mr King möchte wissen, wie viele Tricks der Zauberer machen kann.

____?

Exercise 2 Steve is sick today and can't watch the magician's performance. He is at home talking to his mum. Complete the dialogue. Read his mother's answers first.

Steve: "____?"

Mum: "You must take the medication until you feel better."

Steve: "____?"

Mum: "You can probably go back to school on Wednesday."

Steve: "____?"

Mum: "They are watching the magician's performance at school today.

Steve: "____?"

Mum: I think Sam is knocking at the door. He is bringing your homework.

Steve: "____?"

Mum: "You can do your homework in bed today."

Exercise 1

a)

Which trick / now / do / you
Which trick are you doing now?

not show / us / Why / you / the cards
Why aren't you showing us the cards?

can / you / do / with your hat / What
What can you do with your hat?

behind your back / What / have got / you
What have you got behind your back?

Why / a pink bow / the bunny / has got
Why has the bunny got a pink bow?

b)

Why haven't you got another card trick?
When can you come back? Next week perhaps?
How far can the bunny jump? 2 metres?
Where is the magician? I can't see him.

c)

Where **must** we go after the performance?
When **can** I get the magician's autograph?
When **must** we be back in our classrooms?
Where **can** the bunny be?

d)

Wo kann ich meinen Hut ablegen?
Where can I put my hat?

Wann muss ich fertig sein?
When must I be ready?

Wieso kann ich diesen Tisch nicht benutzen?
Why can't I use this table?

Wie lang sind die Unterrichtsstunden?
How long are the lessons?

e)

Den Direktor interessiert, wie viele Kinder dem Zauberer zuschauen können.
How many children can watch you?

Er möchte wissen, was der Hase gerade im Hut des Zauberers macht.
What is the bunny doing in your hat?

Er fragt, was in dem grossem Korb des Zauberers ist.
What is in your big basket?

Mr King möchte wissen, wie viele Tricks der Zauberer machen kann.
How many tricks can you do?

Exercise 2

Steve: **"How long must I take the medication?"**
Mum: "You must take the medication until you feel better."
Steve: **"When can I go back to school?"**
Mum: "You can probably go back to school on Wednesday."
Steve: **"What are they doing at school today?"**
Mum: "They are watching the magician's performance at school today.
Steve: **"Who is knocking at the door?"**
Mum: "I think Sam is knocking at the door. He is bringing your homework."
Steve: **"Where can I do my homework today?"**
Mum: "You can do your homework in bed today."

ANSWER KEY ANSWER KEY ANSWER KEY

32 *Who/what* as subject or object in questions (Die Fragewörter *who/what* als Subjekt oder Objekt in Fragen)

Who und ***what*** können sowohl Subjekt als auch Objekt in Fragesätzen sein.

1 *Who/what* as subject in questions

Werden ***who*** und ***what*** als Subjekt des Fragesatzes verwendet (Frage: *Wer* oder *was?*), so entfällt das Hilfsverb ***do*** in der Frage. Die Fragestellung entspricht dann der Fragestellung im Deutschen: question word (1) - verb (2) - attribute (3).

1	2	3	1	2	3
Who	*is*	*your best friend?*	**Wer**	ist	dein bester Freund?
Who	*is*	*late for school?*	**Wer**	kommt	zu spät zur Schule?
What	*is*	*your favourite subject?*	**Was**	ist	dein Lieblingsfach?
What	*happens*	*in the story?*	**Was**	geschieht	in der Geschichte?

2 *Who/what* as object in questions

Werden ***who*** und ***what*** als Objekt des Fragesatzes gebraucht (Frage: *Wen/wem* oder *was?*), so muss das Hilfsverb ***do*** ergänzt werden. Fragestellung: question word (1) - auxiliary (2) - subject (3) - verb (4) - attribute (5)

1	2	3	4	5	1	2	3	4
Who	***do***	*you*	*like*	*best?*	**Wen**	magst	du	am liebsten?
Who	***does***	*Jenny*	*look*	*like?*	**Wem**	sieht	Jenny	ähnlich?
What	***does***	*Robert*	*do*	*in his free time?*	**Was**	macht	Robert	in seiner Freizeit?
What	***do***	*British people*	*have*	*for breakfast?*	**Was**	essen	Briten	zum Frühstück?

Ist bereits ein anderes Hilfsverb in der Frage vorhanden, so ist die Umschreibung mit ***do*** nicht mehr notwendig.

1	2	3	4	5	1	2	3	4
What	*can*	*you*	*see*	*in the picture?*	**Was**	kannst	du	auf dem Bild sehen?

Die Fragestellung mit ***do*** fällt uns schwer, da wir im Deutschen kein derartiges Hilfsverb für Fragen brauchen. Überlege dir daher immer genau, ob du nach der Person oder Sache fragst, die etwas tut oder bewirkt *(Wer* oder *was?)* oder ob du nach Personen und Dingen fragst, mit denen etwas getan wird *(Wen/wem* oder *was?)*.
Beispiele: *Who **is** your best friend?/Who **do** you like best?*

Bedenke auch, dass diese Regeln nur für das ***simple present*** gelten. Beim ***present progressive*** verwendest du in der Frage bereits das Hilfsverb ***to be*** und brauchst kein weiteres Hilfsverb mehr: *What **is** she reading?*

EXERCISE 1 What does Linda usually do on Saturdays? Here are some answers. Can you find the questions? Ask for the underlined words.

1 ______________________________?

Linda sleeps late.

2 ______________________________?

Her dog Harry wakes her up and washes her face.

3 ______________________________?

Linda has muesli for breakfast.

4 ______________________________?

Harry hates muesli.

5 ______________________________?

Linda takes some plates out of the cupboard for her family.

6 ______________________________?

She must set the table for her parents and her brother Larry.

EXERCISE 2 Linda has a new friend. She wants to write her an e-mail and ask her some questions. Can you help her with the questions and put them in the right order?

1 wakes / in the morning / up / Who / you

______________________________?

2 have / you / for breakfast / What / do

______________________________?

3 is / your / Who / teacher / favourite

______________________________?

4 to / kind of / What / music / do / listen / you

______________________________?

5 can / Who / you / talk / to / if you have a problem

______________________________?

6 in / What / you / do / do / afternoon / the

______________________________?

Exercise 3 Linda's new friend Lisa is writing her an e-mail. She wants to know many things. Translate the following questions into English.

1 Was liest du gerne?

______________________________?

2 Was ist dein Lieblingsfach?

______________________________?

3 Was magst du nicht?

______________________________?

4 Wie ist der Name deines Hundes?

______________________________?

5 Was kannst du mir über deine Stadt erzählen?

______________________________?

Exercise 4 Put in the right form of the verb **to do** if you need it.

Linda wants to help her mother with the shopping. At the supermarket she asks herself some questions: "What did Mum say yesterday? Who __________ wants to come and have lunch with us today? And what ________ we want to eat for lunch? Who __________ can help me? I have no idea! Let's see ... Oh yes, Mum said that Uncle James would come *(= würde kommen)* to see us. And she wants to make pizza. Okay. What _________ James like to have on his pizza? __________ he like onions? What ____________ he like to drink? Oh dear, this is so difficult *(= schwierig)* ..."

Exercise 5 Put in the right verb forms of **to be, to do, can.**

1 Who ____________ eating an ice cream?
2 Who ____________ they meet every day?
3 Who ____________ their favourite teacher?
4 What ____________ you tell me about this film?
5 What ____________ you like best?
6 Who ____________ help me with my homework?
7 What ____________ your favourite subject?

Exercise 1

1 **Who sleeps late?**
Linda sleeps late.
2 **Who wakes her up and washes her face?**
Her dog Harry wakes her up and washes her face.
3 **What does Linda have for breakfast?**
Linda has muesli for breakfast.
4 **What does Harry hate?**
Harry hates muesli.
5 **What does Linda take out of the cupboard for her family?**
Linda takes some plates out of the cupboard for her family.
6 **What must she do for her parents and her brother Larry?**
She must set the table for her parents and her brother Larry.

Exercise 2

1 wakes / in the morning / up / Who / you
Who wakes you up in the morning?
2 have / you / for breakfast / What / do
What do you have for breakfast?
3 is / your / Who / teacher / favourite
Who is your favourite teacher?
4 to / kind of / What / music / do / listen / you
What kind of music do you listen to?
5 can / Who / you / talk / to / if you have a problem
Who can you talk to if you have a problem?
6 in / What / you / do / do / afternoon / the
What do you do in the afternoon?

Exercise 3

1 Was liest du gerne?
What do you like to read?
2 Was ist dein Lieblingsfach?
What is your favourite subject?
3 Was magst du nicht?
What don't you like?
4 Wie ist der Name deines Hundes?
What is the name of your dog?
5 Was kannst du mir über deine Stadt erzählen?
What can you tell me about your city?

Exercise 4

Linda wants to help her mother with the shopping. At the supermarket she asks herself some questions: "What did Mum say yesterday? Who wants to come and have lunch with us today? And what **do** we want to eat for lunch? Who can help me? I have no idea! Let's see ... Oh yes, Mum said that Uncle James would come (= würde kommen) to see us. And she wants to make pizza. Okay. What **does** James like to have on his pizza? **Does** he like onions? What **does** he like to drink? Oh dear, this is so difficult (= schwierig) ..."

Exercise 5

1 Who **is** eating an ice cream?
2 Who **do** they meet every day?
3 Who **is** their favourite teacher?
4 What **can** you tell me about this film?
5 What **do** you like best?
6 Who **can** help me with my homework?
7 What **is** your favourite subject?

Ordinal numbers and saying the date

Exercise 1 Write the **months** into Chris' birthday calendar. 8 P

Exercise 2 Then listen to the text twice and fill in the **dates** and **names.** 21 P

Exercise 3 After that fill in the **ordinal numbers** as words. 10 P

exercise 3 ordinal numbers (words)	exercise 2 dates	exercise 1 months	exercise 2 names
______	______	*January*	______
fourth	______	______	______
______	*5th*	______	*Max and Matthew*
______	______	*April*	______
______	______	______	______
______	______	______	______
______	______	______	*Grandma*
______	______	*August*	______
______	______	*September*	______
______	______	______	______
______	______	______	______
______	______	______	______

Exercise 4 Chris tells his friends the **date** for his party. What does he say? 4 P

Hi Tom! How are you? Would you like to come to my birthday party on (8th May 2012)

____

______________________________?

Exercise 5 Find the questions for these answers. 8 P

1 What ______________ is it? It's 4.40 pm.

2 ______________ today? Today is 8th May, 2012.

3 ______________ 8th May? It's a Monday.

4 ______________? My birthday is on 8th May.

EXERCISE 6 What does Agnes have to do **first** / **second** / **third** / **fourth** to prepare *(= vorbereiten)* for Chris's birthday party?

__________ she has to ask Chris's sister what kind of present he would like.
__________ she has to get the bus to be at his party on time.
__________ she has to get the present and a birthday card for Chris.
__________ she has to write the birthday card.

4 P

Telling the time

EXERCISE 7 On Monday Chris has to go to many birthday parties. Write down the **times.**

Party #1 starts at

____

Party #2 starts at

____

Party #3 starts at

____

Party #4 starts at

____

Party #5 starts at

____

Party #6 starts at

____

6 P

Adverbs of frequency in statements

Exercise 8 What does Chris normally do on his birthday? Underline the **adverbs of frequency** and make sentences. You also have to put the **verb** into the correct form.

1 to sleep late / normally / on his birthday / Chris

____.

2 often / He / to have / with his family / breakfast

____.

3 to invite / usually / his friends / His mum and dad / to his birthday party

____.

4 on his birthday / a birthday cake / always / to get / He

____.

5 on his birthday / to cry / never / Chris

____.

5 P

Questions with question words and *do/does*

Exercise 9 Connect the **question words** with **do / does** and the rest of the sentence. Write the questions.

When	do / does	she / to ask / so many questions	?
Who		you / this exercise / to like	
What		to like / you	
Why		to want / for dinner / he	
Where		you / to get up	
How		to live / they	

1 ____?

2 ____?

3 ____?

4 ____?

5 ____?

6 ____?

6 P

✓ ↩ ?

Questions with question words and *to be, have got, must, can*

EXERCISE 10 Find the **questions** for these answers.

1 What ______________________? You must clean the house.

2 When ______________________? I've got time tomorrow.

3 When ______________________? We can have dinner at 6 pm.

4 Where ______________________? The folder is in your school bag.

4 P

Who/what as subject or object in questions

EXERCISE 11 Connect the words and write complete **questions.** Then find the correct answers.

Who / **What**	Agnes / to call	1	Agnes is, because she is smiling.
	to ask / her / Chris	2	She phones Chris.
	to answer / Agnes	3	He invites her to his party.
	to be happy / about the invitation	4	She accepts his invitation.
	to happen / at the party	5	Agnes gives Chris a present.

1 ____.

2 ____.

3 ____.

4 ____.

5 ____.

10 P

Mixed Bag

EXERCISE 12 Cross out the odd word out and explain why.

1 to walk / to watch / today / to cross ______________________

2 Monday / November / Wednesday / Friday ______________________

3 who / where / was / when ______________________

4 usually / always / often / here ______________________

5 sit / do / must / can ______________________

10 P

EXERCISE 13 A phone call. Fill in the gaps and find out who the surprise guest *(= Überraschungsgast)* is. Sometimes you must insert **do/does.**

Chris: "Hello Agnes, would you like to come to my birthday party? It's this afternoon."

Agnes: "Yes, thanks for invitation. ______________________ (I / can / what / to get) you as a present? ______________________ (when / I / have to) be there? And most important:______________________ (to bring / can / I) a friend?"

Chris: "Nothing, whenever you want, and to your last question: ______________________ ______________________ (you / who / to want) to bring with you?"

Agnes: "It's a surprise guest. ______________________ (to be / where) the party?"

Chris: "It's in our garden."

Agnes: "______________________ (what / to say / your sister) about the party?"

Chris: "Nothing, she is in London. ______________________ (why / to ask / you)?"

______________________ (what / to think / you), who is the surprise guest?

8 P

EXERCISE 14 ☆ You are writing a letter to your American pen friend and you tell him about your birthday. Write about 6 sentences and use all the words below.

invitation card | present | games | drinks | birthday cake | usually | often | never | sometimes

____

____

____

____

____

____

Auswertung Trage rechts deine Gesamtpunktzahl ein und vergleiche.

☺ 104 – 79 points	😐 78 – 53 points	☹ 52 – 0 points

TOTAL SCORE 104 P

Exercise 1, 2, 3

exercise 3 ordinal numbers (words)	exercise 2 dates	exercise 1 months	exercise 2 names
twelfth	**12th**	January	**Tom**
fourth	**4th**	**February**	**Mum / Mary**
fifth	5th	**March**	Max and Matthew
thirteenth	**13th**	April	**Ann**
thirty-first	**31st**	**May**	**Henry**
third	**3rd**	**June**	**Grandpa**
second	**2nd**	**July**	Grandma
ninth	**9th**	August	**Bee**
nineteenth	**19th**	September	**Aunt Judith**
twentieth	**20th**	**October**	**Uncle Paul**
	?	**November**	**dog / Barky**
sixth	**6th**	**December**	**Dad / Peter**

Exercise 4
Hi Tom! How are you? Would you like to come to my birthday party on **the eighth of May (May the eighth) two thousand and twelve.**

Exercise 5
1 What **time** is it? 2 **What's the date** today? 3 **What day is 8th** May? 4 **When is your birthday?**

Exercise 6
First, she has to ask Chris's sister what kind of present he would like. | **Second,** she has to get the present and a birthday card for Chris. | **Third,** she has to write the birthday card. | **Fourth,** she has to get the bus to be at his party on time.

Exercise 7
Party #1 starts at **five past eleven.** | #2 = **half past twelve** | #3 = **quarter to two** | #4 = **three o'clock** | #5 = **five to five** | #6 = **27 minutes past six**

Exercise 8
1 Chris normally sleeps late on his birthday. 2 He often has breakfast with his family. 3 His mum and dad usually invite his friends to his birthday party. 4 He always gets a birthday cake on his birthday. 5 Chris never cries on his birthday.

Exercise 9
1 When do you get up? 2 Who do you like? 3 What does he want for dinner? 4 Why does she ask so many questions? 5 Where do they live? 6 How do you like this exercise?

Exercise 10
1 What must we (I) do? 2 When have you got time? 3 When can we have dinner? 4 Where is the folder?

Exercise 11
1 Who does Agnes call? – She phones Chris. 2 What does Chris ask her? – He invites her to his party. 3 What does Agnes answer? – She accepts his invitation. 4 Who is happy about the invitation? – Agnes is, because she is smiling. 5 What happens at the party? – Agnes gives Chris a present.

Exercise 12
1 ~~today~~: It is an **adverb** and the other words are **verbs.**
2 ~~November~~: It is a **month** and the other words are **days of the week.**
3 ~~was~~: It is a form of **to be** and the other words are **question words.**
4 ~~here~~: It is an **adverb of place** and the others are **adverbs of frequency.**
5 ~~sit~~: It is a **full verb** and the other words are **auxiliary verbs.**

Exercise 13
What can I get | when do I have to | can I bring | Who do you want | Where is | What does your sister say | Why do you ask | What do you think

ANSWER KEY ANSWER KEY ANSWER KEY

33 Connectives and connective phrases (Konjunktionen und satzverbindende Wendungen)

Connectives oder ***conjunctions*** *(Konjunktionen)* und ***connective phrases*** *(satzverbindende Wendungen)* wie ***and, but, because, first, then, finally*** verbinden Sätze oder Satzteile miteinander.

Conjunctions können in folgende Gruppen eingeteilt werden:

- ***Coordinating conjunctions*** *(beiordnende Konjunktionen)* sind Bindewörter, die grammatisch gleichwertige Sätze, gleichrangige Satzteile, Wortgruppen oder Wörter miteinander verbinden.
- ***Subordinating conjunctions*** *(unterordnende Konjunktionen)* werden benutzt, um einen Nebensatz einem Hauptsatz unterzuordnen.

Connective phrases *(satzverbindende Wendungen)* können die Inhalte eines Satzes oder auch die mehrerer Sätze strukturieren, z. B. in ihrer zeitlichen Abfolge.

1 Coordinating and subordinating conjunctions

And *(und)* und ***but*** *(aber)* sind ***coordinating conjunctions*** *(beiordnende Konjunktionen)*, die gleichwertige Sätze, Satzteile, Wortgruppen oder Wörter einander beiordnen.
And wird bei Aufzählungen, ***but*** wird bei Einschränkungen oder Gegensätzen verwendet:

and:	*Harry*	***and***	*I go to school together.*
	Harry plays the drums,	***and***	*his brother plays the guitar.*
but:	*I like music,*	***but***	*I don't play an instrument.*

Die ***subordinating conjunction*** *(unterordnende Konjunktion)* ***because*** *(weil)* ordnet einem Hauptsatz einen Nebensatz unter und beschreibt eine kausale Beziehung oder Begründung.

because:	*He is happy,*	***because***	*he got a new guitar for his birthday.*

2 Connective phrases

Connective phrases *(satzverbindende Wendungen)* strukturieren Gedanken und Inhalte eines Satzes oder Textes und zeigen Beziehungen zwischen Sätzen oder Absätzen eines Textes auf. Die Ausdrücke ***first, then, finally*** zeigen eine Sequenz bzw. zeitliche Abfolge von Inhalten eines Satzes oder Textes an. Sie stehen meist am Anfang eines Satzes.

- ***First,*** *you mix the dough.*
- ***Then,*** *you roll it out.*
- ***Finally,*** *you put pizza sauce and cheese on it.*

Nach den satzverbindenden Wendungen ***first, then*** und ***finally,*** wird ein Komma gesetzt, ebenso vor ***and*** und ***but,*** wenn diese zwei unabhängige Sätze verbinden. Sind diese jedoch sehr kurz, kann das Komma weggelassen werden.

Exercise 1 **And** or **but?**

1 I like strawberries __________ bananas on my pancakes.

2 Ely does not like carrots, __________ he loves peas.

3 I want to come to your party, __________ I don't have time.

4 She invited me __________ my friend.

5 We went to the zoo, __________ we looked at the zebras.

Exercise 2 Postcard from the lake. Austin writes a postcard to his sister. He is on a camping trip with the Boy Scouts. Fill in the blanks with **and, but** and **because.**

Yesterday, we made a campfire __________ went to bed late. Now we are tired __________ we stayed up so late at night. We wanted to go swimming today, __________ the water in the lake is too cold __________ we forgot our bathing suits. I hope the weather stays nice, __________ there are lots of clouds __________ it already looks like rain. I'm sorry I can't write more __________ we must make sandwiches for lunch now.

Love, Austin

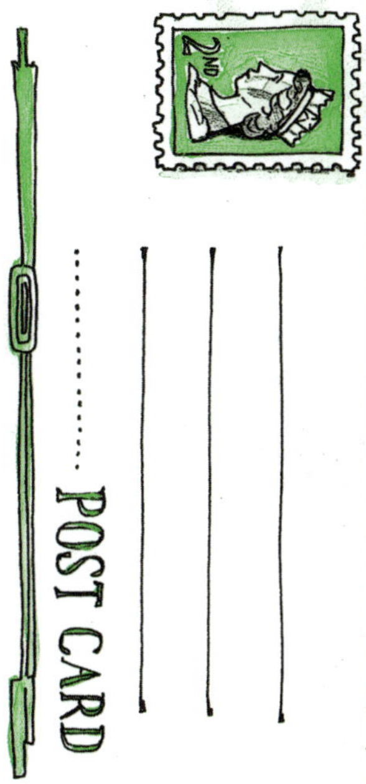

Exercise 3 Put the sentences in the correct order and use **first, then** and **finally** to connect them.

1 Soccer practice

We must put the balls back into the cupboard. We must kick the ball back and forth.
We must run around the field to warm up.

____.

____.

____.

2 Biology class

The pupils must answer questions about the movie. The class watches a movie about insects. The pupils must write down their homework.

____.

____.

____.

3 Dinner

Dad washes the dishes. I set the table. My family and I eat dinner.

____.

____.

____.

Exercise 4 Find the pictures that go together. Then use **and, but** and **because** to connect the sentences under the pictures. Say the sentences out loud.

They visited London

... we were hungry.

We ate a big pizza

... it is raining.

and
because
but

She needed a book

... Edinburgh.

They can't play outside

... the library was closed.

Exercise 1

1 I like strawberries **and** bananas on my pancakes.
2 Ely does not like carrots, **but** he loves peas.
3 I want to come to your party, **but** I don't have time.
4 She invited me **and** my friend.
5 We went to the zoo, **and** we looked at the zebras.

Exercise 2

Yesterday, we made a campfire **and** went to bed late. Now we are tired **because** we stayed up so late at night. We wanted to go swimming today, **but** the water in the lake is too cold **and** we forgot our bathing suits.
I hope the weather stays nice, **but** there are lots of clouds **and** it already looks like rain. I'm sorry I can't write more **because** we must make sandwiches for lunch now.
Love,
Austin

Exercise 3

1 Soccer practice
First, we must run around the field to warm up.
Then, we must kick the ball back and forth.
Finally, we must put the balls back into the cupboard.

2 Biology class
First, the class watches a movie about insects.
Then, the pupils must answer questions about the movie.
Finally, the pupils must write down their homework.

3 Dinner
First, I set the table.
Then, my family and I eat dinner.
Finally, Dad washes the dishes.

Exercise 4

They visited London **and**

We ate a big pizza **because**

She needed a book, **but**

They can't play outside **because**

... we were hungry.

... it is raining.

... Edinburgh.

... the library was closed.

34 *A lot of, much/many, how much /how many* (Mengenangaben mit *a lot of, much/many, how much/how many*)

Much und ***many*** sind ebenso wie ***a lot of*** unbestimmte Mengenangaben. Alle drei werden mit *viel/viele* übersetzt. Sie sind unbestimmt, da man nicht weiß, um wie viel es sich handelt. Alle drei werden unterschiedlich verwendet.

1 *A lot of*

In bejahten Aussagesätzen verwendet man meistens ***a lot of.*** Es kann sowohl mit nicht zählbaren Nomen als auch mit zählbaren Nomen verwendet werden:

Verwendung mit nicht zählbaren Nomen	Verwendung mit zählbaren Nomen
*There is **a lot of** salt in my soup.*	*There are **a lot of** pupils in my class.*

2 *Much* and *many*

In Fragen und verneinten Sätzen verwendet man meist ***much*** und ***many.***

Much wird zusammen mit Nomen verwendet, die **nicht zählbar** sind.

- *How **much** money have you got?*
- *Let me see. Oh no, there isn't **much** money left.*

Many hingegen wird bei Nomen gebraucht, die im Plural stehen und **zählbar** sind:

- *How **many** friends have you got?*
- *I haven't got **many** friends, only two or three.*

Wenn du dir nicht sicher bist, ob du ***much*** oder ***many*** verwenden musst, dann übersetze die Mengenangabe einfach ins Deutsche. ***Much*** wird in der Regel mit *viel* übersetzt und ***many*** mit *viele,* z. B.:

- ***much*** *money* – **viel** Geld
- ***many*** *people* – **viele** Leute

Allerdings gibt es im Englischen einige Nomen, die grammatikalisch im Singular stehen, die aber als Pluralwörter angesehen werden. Hier gilt diese Regel nicht:

- ***much*** *information* – **viele** Informationen

3 *How much* and *how many*

In der Frage können ***how much*** und ***how many*** entweder alleine oder mit einem Nomen stehen. ***How much*** steht mit unzählbaren, ***how many*** mit zählbaren Nomen oder an deren Stelle:

Verwendung mit nicht zählbaren Nomen	Verwendung mit zählbaren Nomen
How much *money does the book cost?*	***How many*** *books have you got?*
How much *does the book cost?*	***How many*** *have you got?*

EXERCISE 1 Fill in **much, many** or **a lot of.**

1 There is not ______________________ water in the swimming pool.

2 How ______________________ brothers and sisters have you got?

3 I didn't get ______________________ e-mails today.

4 I put too ______________________ salt in the soup.

5 How ______________________ plates do we need?

6 How ______________________ people were at the party?

7 How ______________________ ice cream did you eat?

8 There are not ______________________ children in the playground.

9 We did not have ______________________ fun.

10 ______________________ people like dogs.

EXERCISE 2 Translate into English.

1 Herr Schmidt hat viele Katzen.

____

____

2 Er gibt *(= spends ... on)* viel Geld für Futter aus.

____

____

3 Er mag es nicht sehr gerne, wenn der Hund des Nachbarn seine Katzen anbellt.

____

____

4 Verbringt er viel Zeit an seinem Computer?

____

____

5 Nein, er verbringt viel Zeit mit seinen Katzen.

____

____

6 Er hat nicht viele Freunde.

____

____

Exercise 3 Fill in **how much** or **how many.**

1 He needs some money. ______________ does he need?

2 He has got some friends. ______________ has he got?

3 We need some paper. ______________ do we need?

4 ______________ children have you got?

5 ______________ fruit do you eat a day?

6 ______________ English people do you know?

7 ______________ money do you spend on clothes?

8 ______________ times must I tell you that I love you?

9 ______________ chairs are there in our classroom?

10 ______________ plates are there in the cupboard?

11 ______________ work have you got to do?

Exercise 4 **Much** or **many?**

______	CDs	______	juice
______	money	______	lemonade
______	pencils	______	pizzas
______	pounds	______	people
______	fun	______	water
______	trousers	______	glasses
______	butter	______	information

Exercise 5 Translate into German.

1 Many glasses (to drink from): ______________

2 Many glasses (to see with): ______________

Exercise 1

1 There is not **much** water in the swimming pool.
2 How **many** brothers and sisters have you got?
3 I didn't get **many** e-mails today.
4 I put too **much** salt in the soup.
5 How **many** plates do we need?
6 How **many** people were at the party?
7 How **much** ice cream did you eat?
8 There are not **many** children in the playground.
9 We did not have **much** fun.
10 **A lot of** people like dogs.

Exercise 2

1 Herr Schmidt hat viele Katzen.
Mr Schmidt has (got) a lot of cats.
2 Er gibt (= spends ... on) viel Geld für Futter aus.
He spends a lot of money on food.
3 Er mag es nicht sehr gerne, wenn der Nachbarshund seine Katzen anbellt.
He does not like it very much when the neighbours' dog barks at his cats.
4 Verbringt er viel Zeit an seinem Computer?
Does he spend much time at his computer?
5 Nein, er verbringt viel Zeit mit seinen Katzen.
No, he spends a lot of time with his cats.
6 Er hat nicht viele Freunde.
He does not have/has not got many friends.

Exercise 3

1 He needs some money. **How much** does he need?
2 He has got some friends. **How many** has he got?
3 We need some paper. **How much** do we need?
4 **How many** children have you got?
5 **How much** fruit do you eat a day?
6 **How many** English people do you know?
7 **How much** money do you spend on clothes?
8 **How many** times must I tell you that I love you?
9 **How many** chairs are there in our classroom?
10 **How many** plates are there in the cupboard?
11 **How much** work have you got to do?

Exercise 4

many CDs	**much** juice
much money	**much** lemonade
many pencils	**many** pizzas
many pounds	**many** people
much fun	**much** water
many trousers	**many** glasses
much butter	**much** information

Exercise 5

many glasses kann heißen:
1 viele Gläser (Singular: a glass)
2 viele Brillen (Singular: a pair of glasses)

Glasses (= Brille) und **trousers** sind Nomen, die im Englischen nur im Plural vorkommen.

35 *Some* and *any/no* in statements, negatives and questions (*Some* und *any/no* in Aussagen, Verneinungen und Fragen)

Wenn man eine unbestimmte Menge oder Anzahl von etwas ausdrücken möchte, benutzt man im Englischen ***some*** oder ***any.***

1 *Some* and *any* in positive and negative statements

Some und ***any*** werden mit Nomen im Plural oder unzählbaren Nomen verwendet. ***Some*** steht im bejahten Aussagesatz, ***any*** steht im verneinten Aussagesatz:

*There are **some** biscuits (= Plural) in the box.*	Es sind **ein paar** Plätzchen in der Schachtel.
*There are**n't any** pears (= Plural).*	Es gibt **keine** Birnen.
*We must buy **some** milk.*	Wir müssen **(etwas)** Milch *(= unzählbar)* kaufen.
*We have**n't** got **any** butter.*	Wir haben **keine** Butter. *(= unzählbar)*

2 *Some* und *any* in questions

Die Verwendung von ***some*** und ***any*** richtet sich nach der Art des Fragesatzes. ***Some*** wird in Fragesätzen verwendet, auf die man eine **positive Antwort** erwartet, bzw. bei **Bitten** oder **Angeboten.**

*Can I have **some** milk, please?*	Kann ich bitte **(etwas)** Milch haben?
*Would you like **some** tea?*	Möchtest du **(etwas)** Tee?

Any wird in **offenen Fragesätzen** verwendet, deren Antwort Ja oder Nein lauten kann:

*Have we got **any** lemonade?*	Haben wir (noch) Limonade?
*Are there **any** sweets in the cupboard?*	Sind (noch) Bonbons im Schrank?

Aufgepasst, häufig werden ***some*** und ***any*** aber nicht mit übersetzt!

*I have got **some** time now.*	Ich habe nun Zeit.
*Have you got **any** questions?*	Hast du / Haben Sie Fragen?

3 *Some* und *any* without following noun

Wenn das Nomen im Fragesatz bereits genannt wurde, können ***some*** und ***any*** im Antwortsatz allein stehen.

*Is there **any** milk left?*	Ist noch **(etwas)** Milch da?
*No, there isn't **any.***	Nein, da ist **keine** (Milch).
*Would you like **some** tea, Anne?*	Anne, möchtest du/möchten Sie **(etwas)** Tee?
*No, thanks. I've still got **some.***	Nein danke. Ich habe noch **welchen/Tee.**

4 *No /not any*

In der Verneinung steht meist ***not any*** *(kein / keine)*. ***No*** wird seltener verwendet.

*I have**n't** got **any** time.* *I have **no** time.*	Ich habe **keine** Zeit.

Exercise 1 Underline the correct form: **some** or **any.**

1 There's *some / any* tea in my cup, but I haven't got *some / any* sugar.

2 We must buy *some / any* tomatoes for Grandma because she hasn't got *some / any* in her garden.

3 You can't eat *some / any* more ice cream; there must be *some / any* left for your Dad.

4 I'd like to buy *some / any* posters for my room, but I haven't got *some / any* pocket money left.

Exercise 2 Look at the list. Write down what she **has / hasn't got** for her birthday party.

1	CDs	✓	movies	✗
2	chocolate crispies	✓	crisps	✗
3	beer	✗	orange juice	✓

1 Mary has got *some* CDs, but she hasn't got *any* movies.

2 She has got ______________________________

3 ______________________________

Exercise 3 Fill in the correct word: **some** or **any.**

Assistant: "Hello. Can I help you?"

Customer: "Yes, please. I'm looking for __________ pink sunglasses."

Assistant: "I'm sorry. We haven't got __________ pink sunglasses.

What about __________ red or blue sunglasses?"

Customer: "No, thanks. I don't want __________ other colour."

Exercise 4 Complete these sentences with **some** or **any** and the correct noun from the boxes.

pet food | pets | presents | time

1 I can't do my homework because I haven't got ______________________________.

2 Sarah must buy ______________________________ for her rabbits.

3 I've got two dogs and a parrot. Have you got ______________________________?

4 It's my birthday today and I've got ______________________________.

Exercise 5 Put in the correct word: **some, any** or **no.**

1 Have you got _________ books about ghosts? – Yes, of course. There are _________ funny books on the shelf on the right.

2 Aren't there _________ mistakes in your test? – Yes, that's right.

3 Would you like _________ more biscuits? – Yes, please. I haven't got _________ like these at home.

4 I can't find my purse. Can you lend me _________ money? – Yes, of course. I've got _________.

5 We haven't got _________ tea today.

6 I don't want _________ mice in my house.

7 The house has got _________ garden, so the we can't play _________ games outside.

8 I think it's a good idea to buy _________ pictures for the living room. Buy _________ new furniture and the room will look lovely. But don't buy _________ cheap things.

Exercise 6 Anna and her friend Mary from London would like to have a picnic. Anna's mum asks what they need for the picnic. Help Anna to translate.

Mum: „Möchte Mary Saft oder Limonade?"

Anna: "*Would you* _________________________________?"

Mary: "I'd like *some* orange juice, please."

Anna: „*Sie* _________________________________."

Mum: „Möchte sie Käse- oder Schinkenbrote?"

Anna: "_________________________________?"

Mary: "No thanks, I don't need *any* sandwiches."

Anna: „_________________________________."

Mum: „Wir haben Bananen, Birnen und Orangen, aber wir haben keine Äpfel."

Anna: "_________________________________."

Mary: "That's OK. We can make *some* fruit salad."

Anna: „_________________________________."

Exercise 1

1 There's **some/any** tea in my cup, but I haven't got **some/any** sugar.
2 We must buy **some/any** tomatoes for Grandma because she hasn't got **some/any** in her garden.
3 You can't eat **some/any** more ice cream; there must be **some/any** left for your Dad.
4 I'd like to buy **some/any** posters for my room, but I haven't got **some/any** pocket money left.

Exercise 2

1 Mary has got **some** CDs, but she hasn't got **any** movies.
2 She has got **some** chocolate crispies, but she hasn't **any** crisps.
3 She hasn't got **any** beer, but she has got **some** orange juice.

Exercise 3

Assistant: "Hello. Can I help you?"
Customer: "Yes, please. I'm looking for **some** pink sunglasses."
Assistant: "I'm sorry. We haven't got **any** pink sunglasses. What about **some** red or blue sunglasses?"
Customer: "No, thanks. I don't want **any** other colour."

Exercise 4

1 I can't do my homework because I haven't got **any time.**
2 Sarah must buy **some pet food** for her rabbits.
3 I've got two dogs and a parrot. Have you got **any pets?**
4 It's my birthday today and I've got **some presents.**

Exercise 5

1 Have you got **any** books about ghosts?
Yes, of course. There are **some** funny books on the shelf on the right.
2 Aren't there **any** mistakes in your test?
Yes, that's right.
3 Would you like **some** more biscuits?
Yes, please. I haven't got **any** like these at home.
4 I can't find my purse. Can you lend me **some** money?
Yes, of course. I've got **some.**
5 We haven't got **any** tea today.
6 I don't want **any** mice in my house.
7 The house has got **no** garden, so we can't play **any** games outside.
8 I think it's a good idea to buy **some** pictures for the living room. Buy **some** new furniture and the room will look lovely. But don't buy **any** cheap things.

Exercise 6

Mum: „Möchte Mary Saft oder Limonade?“
Anna: **"Would you like some juice or (some) lemonade?"**
Mary: "I'd like **some** orange juice, please."
Anna: **„Sie möchte Orangensaft.“**
Mum: „Möchte sie Käse- oder Schinkenbrote?“
Anna: **"Would you like some cheese or (some) ham sandwiches?"**
Mary: "No thanks, I don't need **any** sandwiches."
Anna: **„Sie braucht keine Butterbrote."**
Mum: „Wir haben Bananen, Birnen und Orangen, aber wir haben keine Äpfel.“
Anna: **"We've got some bananas, (some) pears and (some) oranges, but we haven't got any apples."**
Mary: "That's OK. We can make **some** fruit salad."
Anna: **„Das ist okay. Wir können Obstsalat machen.“**

ANSWER KEY ANSWER KEY ANSWER KEY

36 The simple past of regular verbs (Die einfache Vergangenheit regelmäßiger Verben)

Das ***simple past*** *(einfache Vergangenheit)* drückt aus, dass Ereignisse oder Tätigkeiten in der Vergangenheit stattgefunden haben und zu Ende gebracht wurden bzw. abgeschlossen sind. Man benutzt es beispielsweise, um von Erlebnissen in der Vergangenheit zu erzählen. Dabei kommen häufig Signalwörter wie ***yesterday, four days ago, last week, in 2010*** etc. vor. Die Formen des ***simple past*** sind für alle Personen gleich.

1 Regular verb forms

Bei den ***regular verb forms*** *(regelmäßige Verben)* wird das ***simple past*** gebildet, indem man ***-ed*** an den Infinitiv ohne ***to*** anfügt.

*Yesterday I **walked** to school.*	Gestern **ging** ich zu Fuß zur Schule.
*It **rained** all day.*	Es **regnete** den ganzen Tag.
*My parents **watched** a film yesterday evening.*	Meine Eltern **schauten** gestern Abend einen Film.

2 The pronunciation

Für die Aussprache ist ausschlaggebend, welcher Laut am Ende des Infinitivs hörbar ist. An ihn wird die Endung ***-ed*** angefügt.

Nach stimmhaften Konsonanten (z. B. **b, d, m, n, w**) und Vokalen spricht man die Endung wie ein [d] aus, z. B. *show**ed*** [d].
Nach stimmlosen Konsonanten (z. B. **t, p, k, s**) spricht man ein [t], z. B. *talk**ed*** [t].
Nach **d** und **t** am Ende des Infinitivs spricht man [ɪd], z. B. *start**ed*** [ɪd], *need**ed*** [ɪd].

3 The spelling

Drei Regeln sind beim ***spelling*** (bei der Schreibung) zu beachten:

Nach kurzem betontem Vokal wird der Konsonant am Verbende **verdoppelt.**	*to stop – sto**pped*** *to swap – swa**pped***
Ein stummes **-e** am Verbende fällt weg. Das heißt, die Endung weist dann **nur ein -e** statt zwei auf.	*to love – lov**ed*** *to hope – hop**ed*** *to use – us**ed***
Verben, die im Infinitiv die Endung Konsonant + y aufweisen, haben die Endung ***-ied.*** Aber: Bei Vokal + y am Verbende bleibt die Endung ***-yed.***	*to try – tr**ied*** *to worry – worr**ied*** *to play – pla**yed*** *to stay – sta**yed***

☞ Auch bei ***cycled*** und ***chased*** erscheint nur ein ***-e*** in der Endung des ***simple past.*** Denn die Regel besagt: Das stumme ***-e*** am Ende des Infinitivs fällt weg.

Exercise 1 Listen to verbs in the **simple past** and put them into the right lists. Which sound can you hear at the end of each form?

[d]	[t]	[ɪd]
played		*hated*

Exercise 2 A word snake. Can you find the **simple past forms?** Write them down in the right lists and add the **infinitive forms,** too.

double consonant	silent e *(stummes e)*	-y – -ied
to stop – stopped	*to examine – examined*	

Exercise 3 Which signal words for the **simple past** can you find? But be careful: two of them are signal words for a different tense.

tersyeayd *yesterday*

satl eewk ______

wot adsy oga ______

llyausu ______

lats adyMno ______

awysla ______

teehr tesmniu goa ______

na ourh gao ______

______ and ______ are **not** signal words for the simple past.

They are signal words for the ______.

Exercise 4 John's first day at school. What a day! Put these verbs in their **simple past forms.**

to finish   to play   to start   to stay

Last week John had his first day at his new school in Liverpool. It ________________ at 8.45 in the morning and ________________ at 3.30 in the afternoon. After that he ________________ in the playground with his new friends and they ________________ basketball.

to fetch   to land   to try   to turn

Tim, a boy from his team, ________________ the ball and ________________ towards John. John ________________ to catch it but he wasn't fast enough. The next moment he ________________ on the ground and hurt his knee.

to collect   to help   to phone   to stop

The boys ________________ their match and ________________ John, of course. They ________________ his mum and she ________________ her son. Was John angry? Of course not. Now he had some new friends in Liverpool.

Exercise 5 What goes together? Make sentences in the **simple past.**

the English teacher	to cycle	all day
a pupil	to chase	the class a map of Scotland
her mother	to rain	a mouse
their cat	to ask	lots of good questions in class
it	to show	to her office

(the English teacher → to show → ?)

1 *The English teacher showed* ________________.

2 ________________.

3 ________________.

4 ________________.

5 ________________.

Exercise 1

[d]	[t]	[ɪd]
played	talked	hated
tried	worked	started
opened	looked	shouted
rained	walked	needed

Exercise 2

double consonant	silent -e (stummes -e)	-y – -ied
to stop – stopped	to examine – examined	to carry – carried
to clap – clapped	to hate – hated	to try – tried
to grab – grabbed	to love – loved	to copy – copied
to plan – planned	to like – liked	to cry – cried
to quiz – quizzed	to invite – invited	to empty – emptied

Exercise 3

yesterday	last week
two days ago	usually
last Monday	always
three minutes ago	an hour ago

Usually and **always** are not signal words for the simple past. They are signal words for the **simple present.**

Achte darauf, dass im Englischen **ago** am Ende steht, z. B. **two years ago.** Im Deutschen sagt man dagegen: vor zwei Jahren.

Exercise 4

Last week John had his first school day at his new school in Liverpool. It **started** at 8.45 in the morning and **finished** at 3.30 in the afternoon. After that he **stayed** in the playground with his new friends and they **played** basketball.

Bei **stayed** und **played** bleibt das **-y** im **simple past** bestehen, da im Infinitiv ein Vokal vor dem **-y** steht.

Tim, a boy from his team, **fetched** the ball and **turned** towards John. John **tried** to catch it but he wasn't fast enough. The next moment he **landed** on the ground and hurt his knee.

The boys **stopped** their match and **helped** John, of course. They **phoned** his mum and she **collected** her son. Was John angry? Of course not. Now he had some new friends in Liverpool.

Hinweis für die Aussprache: started, landed und **collected** werden am Ende mit [ɪd] ausgesprochen.

Exercise 5

the English teacher	to cycle	all day
a pupil	to chase	the class a map of Scotland
her mother	to rain	a mouse
their cat	to ask	lots of good questions in class
it	to show	to her office

1 The English teacher **showed** the class a map of Scotland.
2 A pupil **asked** lots of good questions in class.
3 Her mother **cycled** to her office.
4 Their cat **chased** a mouse.
5 It **rained** all day.

37 The simple past with *to be* and *to have/have got* (Die einfache Vergangenheit mit *to be* und *to have/have got*)

1 The simple past with *to be*

Im ***simple past*** gibt es zwei Verbformen von ***to be:*** Mit ***I / he / she / it*** benutzt man ***was.*** Mit ***you / we / they*** wird ***were*** verwendet.

In der verneinten Form wird ***not*** dem Verb nachgestellt, bzw. als ***short form*** *(Kurzform)* mit ***-n't*** direkt an das Verb angehängt.

positive statements	negative statements (short forms)
*I **was** in class 4a last year.*	*I **wasn't** in class 4a last year*
*You **were** a clever pupil.*	*You **weren't** a clever pupil.*
*He/She **was** a nice neighbour.*	*He/She **wasn't** a nice neighbour.*
*We **were** in Exeter in 2011.*	*We **weren't** in Exeter in 2011.*
*You **were** great friends.*	*You **weren't** great friends.*
*They **were** very funny yesterday.*	*They **weren't** very funny yesterday.*

Bei Entscheidungsfragen und Kurzantworten mit ***was/were*** wird kein ***did*** benötigt. Wie auch bei Entscheidungsfragen im ***simple present*** steht das Verb am Anfang, gefolgt vom Subjekt des Satzes. Die Kurzantwort greift das Personalpronomen ***I, you, he, she, it, we, they*** und das Verb ***was/were*** wieder auf.

question	short answer
***Were** you at Exmouth primary school last year?*	*Yes, I **was.**/Yes, we **were.*** *No, I **wasn't.**/No, we **weren't.***
***Was** your brother Kevin happy?*	*Yes, he **was.**/No, he **wasn't.***

2 The simple past with *to have*

Das ***simple past*** von ***to have*** ist unregelmäßig und lautet in allen Personen (Singular und Plural) ***had.*** Für die Verneinung verwendet man ***didn't*** und den Infinitiv ***have*** (ohne ***to***). ***Have got*** wird im ***simple past*** zu ***had.***

positive statements	negative statements (short forms)
*I/you/we/they **had** some good friends.*	*I/you/we/they **didn't have** any good friends.*
*He/She/It **had** enough to drink.*	*He/She/It **didn't have** enough to drink.*

Entscheidungsfragen werden mit ***did*** am Satzanfang eingeleitet, gefolgt vom Subjekt des Satzes und dem Vollverb ***have*** (ohne ***to***) im Infinitiv.

question	short answer
***Did** you have good teachers at school?*	*Yes, I **did.** /Yes, we **did.*** *No, I **didn't.**/No, we **didn't.***
***Did** Sam have time for his homework yesterday?*	*Yes, he **did.**/No, he **didn't.***

Exercise 1 A postcard from France. Jane got a postcard from her friend Joe. A week later Jane talks to her mother about the postcard. Fill in the right **simple past forms.**

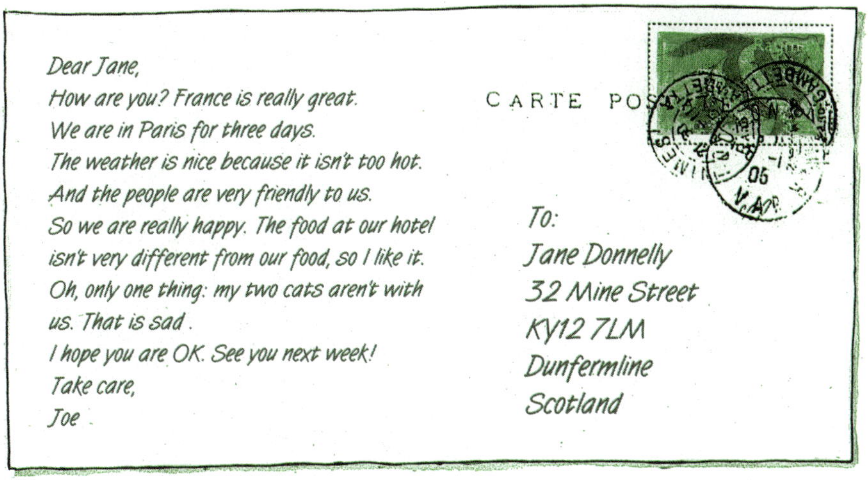

Jane: "Look Mum, Joe sent me a postcard. For him and his family France ___________ really great. They ___________ in Paris for three days and they were lucky with the weather. It ___________ nice because it ___________ too hot. He says that the people ___________ very friendly to them, so they ___________ very happy."

Mum: "What else does he write? ___________ he at Versailles, too?"

Jane: "Sorry, no idea. But the food at their hotel ___________ too different from English food, he writes. But he missed his cats. They ___________ on holiday with them, of course. That ___________ sad for him."

Exercise 2 When Joe and Jane are back at school, Jane asks him lots of questions. Write down the questions with **was/were** and Joe's short answers.

Jane: you / at Versailles / too? "___________________________"

Joe: "No, ___________________. There wasn't enough time for that."

Jane: in the Louvre / your parents? "___________________________"

Joe: "Yes, ___________________. But I ___________________."

Jane: a long trip / it / not / to Paris? "___________________________"

Joe: "No, ___________________. The trip by train was very fast!"

Exercise 3 In the afternoon Joe meets his friend Sam. They talk about Paris, too. Put in the missing words: positive (+) or negative (–) statements, questions or short answers with **to be/have (got)** in the **simple past.**

Sam: "Hi Joe, nice to see you again! Where ____________ you last week? ____________ you at home? I tried to phone you on Monday but then I ____________ (–) time to phone you again."

Joe: "Oh, don't worry because I ________________ (–) at home. We ________________ (+) in Paris for a week and I ________________ (–) my mobile with me."

Sam: "Paris sounds great. ____________ you and your family ____________ a good holiday?"

Joe: "Yes, we ____________. Of course there ____________ (–) enough time to see everything. But we ____________ (+) a nice hotel in the city centre and from there it ____________ (–) far to the tourist attractions."

Sam: "____________ you ____________ time to go shopping?"

Joe: "Yes, I ____________. And I've got something for you: a little Eiffel Tower. Here you are."

Exercise 4 Joe's dad Lewis calls his friend Martin on his mobile. Listen to the dialogue and put these holiday activities in the correct order.

Die unregelmäßigen Formen der einfachen Vergangenheit sollten für diese Aufgabe bereits bekannt sein (→ Modul 38).

	They went to the Eiffel Tower.
	When they arrived in Paris, they weren't tired.
	Joe bought some postcards.
	Joe was too tired to go to the Louvre.
1	The family had a good trip to Paris by train.
	Lewis had his camera with him and took lots of photos.
	Joe and his family had coffee at Montmartre.

Exercise 1

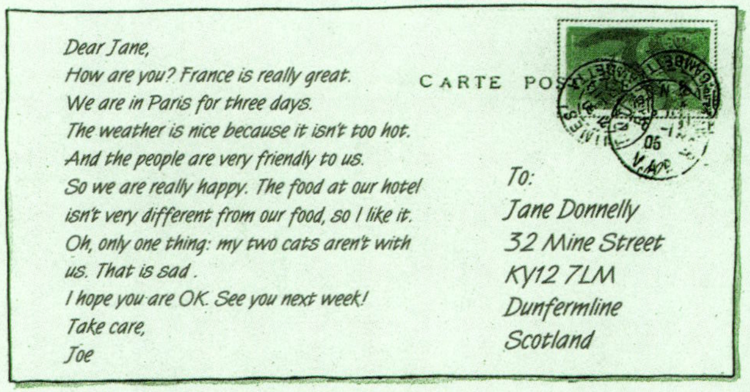

Jane: "Look Mum, Joe sent me a postcard. For him and his family France **was** really great. They **were** in Paris for three days and they **were** lucky with the weather. It **was** nice because it **wasn't / was not** too hot. He says that the people **were** very friendly to them, so they **were** very happy."

Mum: "What else does he write? **Was** he at Versailles, too?"

Jane: "Sorry, no idea. But the food at their hotel **wasn't / was not** too different from English food, he writes. But he missed his cats. They **weren't / were not** on holiday with them, of course. That **was** sad for him."

Exercise 2

Jane: **"Were you at Versailles, too?"**

Joe: "No, **I wasn't / we weren't.** There wasn't enough time for that."

Jane: **"Were your parents in the Louvre?"**

Joe: "Yes, **they were.** But I **wasn't.**"

Jane: **"Wasn't it a long trip to Paris?"**

Joe: "No, **it wasn't.** The trip by train was very fast!"

Beachte, dass im Englischen **yes** oder **no** alleine meist unhöflich klingt. Deshalb verwendet man **short answers.**

Wiederhole bei dieser Gelegenheit auch noch einmal die bereits gelernten **short answers** mit **can** (→ Modul 17), **have got / has got** (→ Modul 14) und den Formen von **to be** im **simple present** (→ Modul 25) und **present progressive** (→ Modul 23).

Exercise 3

Sam: "Hi Joe, nice to see you again! Where **were** you last week? **Were** you at home? I tried to phone you on Monday but then I **didn't have / did not have** time to phone you again."

Joe: "Oh, don't worry because I **wasn't / was not** at home. We **were** in Paris for a week and I **didn't have / did not have** my mobile with me."

Sam: "Paris sounds great. **Did** you and your family **have** a good holiday?"

Joe: "Yes, we **did.** Of course there **wasn't / was not** enough time to see everything. But we **had** a nice hotel in the city centre and from there it **wasn't / was not** far to the tourist attractions."

Sam: "**Did** you **have** time to go shopping?"

Joe: "Yes, I **did.** And I've got something for you: a little Eiffel Tower. Here you are."

Exercise 4

1	The family had a good trip to Paris by train.
2	When they arrived in Paris they weren't tired.
3	Joe bought some postcards.
4	They went to the Eiffel Tower.
5	Joe was too tired to go to the Louvre.
6	Joe and his family had coffee at Montmartre.
7	Lewis had his camera with him and took lots of photos.

Lies dir zu Beginn jeder **listening exercise** die Angabe immer zwei Mal genau durch. So kannst du dann viel schneller die Aufgabe lösen und kommst nicht in Zeitnot. Dies ist vor allem bei Prüfungen wichtig.

ANSWER KEY ANSWER KEY ANSWER KEY

38 The simple past of irregular verbs (Die einfache Vergangenheit unregelmäßiger Verben)

Neben der regelmäßigen Bildung des ***simple past*** mit ***-ed*** gibt es im Englischen auch zahlreiche Verben, deren einfache Vergangenheit unregelmäßig gebildet wird.
Die unregelmäßigen Verben des ***simple past*** werden am besten auswendig gelernt.
Die Formen sind für alle Personen gleich.

1 Simple past: irregular verbs

Folgende Übersicht zeigt die wichtigsten unregelmäßigen Formen des ***simple past.***

infinitive	simple present	simple past
to begin	*begin / begins*	***began***
to choose	*choose / chooses*	***chose***
to come	*come / comes*	***came***
to do	*do / does*	***did***
to drink	*drink / drinks*	***drank***
to get	*get / gets*	***got***
to give	*give / gives*	***gave***
to go	*go / goes*	***went***
to have	*have / has*	***had***
to make	*make / makes*	***made***
to meet	*meet / meets*	***met***
to run	*run / runs*	***ran***
to say	*say / says*	***said***
to see	*see / sees*	***saw***
to sing	*sing / sings*	***sang***
to take	*take / takes*	***took***
to tell	*tell / tells*	***told***
to understand	*understand / understands*	***understood***
to write	*write / writes*	***wrote***

2 Simple past: the forms of *to be*

Das englische Verb ***to be*** hat in der Vergangenheit auch unregelmäßige Formen. Im Gegensatz zu anderen unregelmäßigen Verben gibt es zwei Formen der Vergangenheit: ***was*** und ***were*** (→ Modul 37). Es hat auch verschiedene Frage- und Negativformen.

positive	negative	question
*I **was.***	*I **was not.***	***Was** I?*
*You **were.***	*You **were not.***	***Were** you?*
*He **was.***	*He **was not.***	***Was** he?*
*She **was.***	*She **was not.***	***Was** she?*
*It **was.***	*It **was not.***	***Was** it?*
*We **were.***	*We **were not.***	***Were** we?*
*They **were.***	*They **were not.***	***Were** they?*

Exercise 1 Underline the verbs in the **simple past** and write down the **infinitives.** Then decide: are they **regular** or **irregular?**

	infinitive	regular	irregular
Yesterday, Peter and I took a walk in the park.	to take	______	✗
He walked all the way to Alaska.	______	______	______
They were at the swimming pool and not at the cinema.	______	______	______
My teacher told me what to do.	______	______	______
Last Saturday I helped my father.	______	______	______
You gave her the book, didn't you?	______	______	______
We watched a quiz show on TV.	______	______	______
I did my homework in the afternoon.	______	______	______

Exercise 2 Complete with **was** or **were** and the correct form of the verbs in brackets.

1 Mary was in the shower when I called (to call) her.

2 My grandparents ______ with me when I ______________ (to visit) London last year.

3 Peter, Wendy and Daniel ______ at home and ______________ (to watch) a movie together.

4 When ______ you and Mary-Ann at the shopping centre?

5 I ______ very tired and so I ____________ (to go) to bed early.

6 When my brother ________ little, he ________ always so happy when I ___________ (to play) with him.

7 Last year, my teachers __________ not very nice. They always _____________ (to give) us a lot of homework. I only ___________ (to like) Mr Smith. He _______ my German teacher and we ___________ (to have) a lot of fun together.

Exercise 3 Translate and put the verbs into the correct **simple past** form:

sagen	to say	said
erzählen	______	______
bekommen	______	______
gehen	______	______
nehmen	______	______

Exercise 4 Read the text about Robert's week and rewrite it in the **simple past.**

On Sunday, Robert and his family visit a fun park together. They have a lot of fun.
On Monday, Robert goes to school and does a difficult test.
On Tuesday, he sees his favourite uncle Tommy and he tells him jokes.
On Wednesday, Robert and his mother make apple cake.
On Thursday, his father takes him to see a movie.
On Friday, he does the shopping for the weekend.
On Saturday, he gets a lot of presents because it's his birthday.

What a week!

On Sunday, Robert and his family visited a fun park together. They had a lot of fun.
On Monday, ______________________________
____
____
____
____
____
____
____
____

Exercise 5 Find the correct forms of the infinitives in the **simple past.** Use the following letters: a – a – a – a – a – d – d – d – d – d – e – e – e – e – e – e – g – g – h – i – i – i – k – l – l – l – l – m – n – n – n – n – o – r – s – s – s – t – t – t – v – w – w

to make	*made*	to see	______
to listen	______	to sing	______
to have	______	to live	______
to run	______	to go	______
to like	______	to get	______

Exercise 1

	infinitive	regular	irregular
Yesterday, Peter and I **took** a walk in the park.	**to take**		✗
He **walked** all the way to Alaska.	**to walk**	✗	
They **were** at the swimming pool and not at the cinema.	**to be**		✗
My teacher **told** me what to do.	**to tell**		✗
Last Saturday I **helped** my father.	**to help**	✗	
You **gave** her the book, didn't you?	**to give**		✗
We **watched** a quiz show on TV.	**to watch**	✗	
I **did** my homework in the afternoon.	**to do**		✗

Exercise 2

1 Mary **was** in the shower when I **called** her.
2 My grandparents **were** with me when I **visited** London last year.
3 Peter, Wendy and Daniel **were** at home and **watched** a movie together.
4 When **were** you and Mary-Ann at the shopping centre?
5 I **was** very tired and so I **went** to bed early.
6 When my brother **was** little, he **was** always so happy when I **played** with him.
7 Last year, my teachers **were** not very nice. They always **gave** us a lot of homework. I only **liked** Mr Smith. He **was** my German teacher and we **had** a lot of fun together.

Exercise 3

sagen	**to say**	**said**
erzählen	**to tell**	**told**
bekommen	**to get**	**got**
gehen	**to go**	**went**
nehmen	**to take**	**took**

Exercise 4

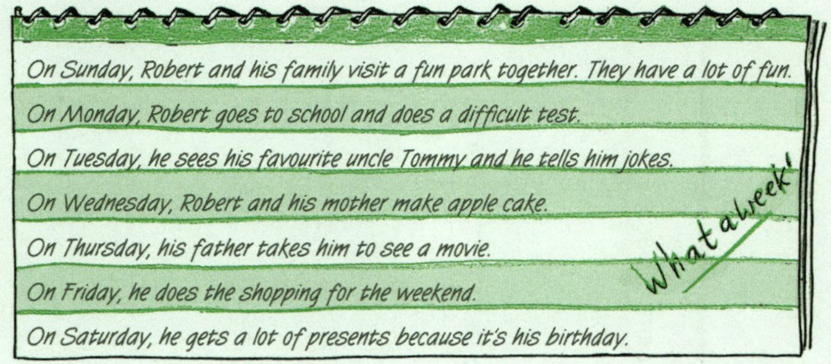

On Sunday, Robert and his family **visited** a fun park together. They **had** a lot of fun.
On Monday, Robert **went** to school and **did** a difficult test.
On Tuesday, he **saw** his favourite uncle Tommy and he **told** him jokes.
On Wednesday, Robert and his mother **made** apple cake.
On Thursday, his father **took** him to see a movie.
On Friday, he **did** the shopping for the weekend.
On Saturday, he **got** a lot of presents because it **was** his birthday.

Exercise 5

to make	**made**	to see	**saw**
to listen	**listened**	to sing	**sang**
to have	**had**	to live	**lived**
to run	**ran**	to go	**went**
to like	**liked**	to get	**got**

ANSWER KEY ANSWER KEY ANSWER KEY

39 The simple past in negatives and questions with *did/didn't* (Die einfache Vergangenheit in Verneinungen und Fragen mit *did/didn't*)

1 Negative statements

Das ***simple past*** *(einfache Vergangenheit)* wird wie das ***simple present*** *(einfaches Präsens)* mit dem Hilfsverb ***to do (didn't)*** und dem Infinitiv des Vollverbs verneint.

- *Mary **didn't play** tennis yesterday morning.*
- *Mary and Peter **didn't eat** any ice cream at the party last night.*

Auch hier gibt es ***long forms*** *(Langformen)* für den schriftlichen Gebrauch und ***short forms*** *(Kurzformen)* für Gespräche:

personal pronouns	long forms	short forms
I You He/She/It We You They	***did not** play tennis.*	***didn't** play tennis.*

Die Vergangenheit ist bereits in der Hilfsverbform ***didn't*** enthalten. Das Vollverb steht bei der Verneinung immer in der Infinitivform:

*Mary play**ed** tennis.* ⇔ *Mary **didn't** play tennis.*

Vergangenheit

Wie im ***simple present*** stehen die Adverbien der Häufigkeit wie ***usually, often, normally*** zwischen dem Hilfsverb und dem Vollverb.

- Mary and Peter ***didn't*** often ***watch*** TV last week.

2 Questions and short answers

Bei Fragen im ***simple past*** werden – genauso wie bei Fragen im ***simple present*** – das Subjekt und das Hilfsverb miteinander vertauscht. Um nicht unhöflich zu sein, antwortet man auch im ***simple past*** nicht nur mit ***Yes/No,*** sondern meist mit einer ***short answer.***

simple present	simple past
*Mary play**s** cards*	*Mary play**ed** cards yesterday.*
***Does** Mary play cards?*	***Did** Mary play cards yesterday?*
Yes, she does.	***Yes, she did.***
No, she doesn't.	***No, she didn't.***

Die Vergangenheit ist bereits in der Hilfsverbform ***did/didn't*** enthalten. Das Vollverb steht bei Fragen immer in der Infinitivform:

*Mary **broke** the cup.* ⇔ ***Did** Mary **break** the cup?*

Vergangenheit

EXERCISE 1 Mary and Peter are playing a game: Underline the correct answer.

1 The Romans *lived/didn't live* in Egypt *(= Ägypten)*.
2 Our grandparents *took/didn't take* the bus to school.
3 In the 16th century Shakespeare *wrote/didn't write* the play *Romeo and Juliet*.
4 The Germans *watched/didn't watch* colour TV in the 1920s.
5 Robert Pattinson *played/didn't play* Edward in *Twilight*.

EXERCISE 2 Mary and Peter are having an argument. Find out Peter's excuses and connect the sentences.

Mary: "Hi Peter, you didn't

1 call me last night."
2 say 'Goodbye' after our History class yesterday."
3 give me back my £5 last Sunday."
4 come to my birthday party."

Peter: "I'm so sorry Mary, but I didn't

a find my invitation.
b get my pocket money.
c have your telephone number."
d see that you were there."

EXERCISE 3 Mary is telling Peter about a rock concert. Make **questions** and **short answers** with these words. Use your own ideas for the negative short answers.

1 you / did / to the concert / to go / by bus ? (–)

Did you ______________________________

No, I didn't. I rode my bike there. ______________________________

2 did / to sing / the band leader / your favourite song ? (+)

____

3 the musicians / funny clothes / did / to wear ? (–)

____

4 did / to go to the concert / you / with your friends ? (–)

____

5 you / all the lyrics *(= Liedtexte)* / did / to know ? (+)

____

Exercise 4 What did Mary do? Fill in the correct **simple past forms** of the verbs and **short answers.**

Peter: "Mary, where were you yesterday afternoon?"

Mary: "Ha, you'll never find out where I was yesterday!"

Peter: "Hmmm, let's see. ______________ you ______________ (to meet) any friends there?"

Mary: "No, I ______________. I ______________ (to go) there with my Dad."

Peter: "So you ______________ (not, to see) any other people there?"

Mary: "That's not what I ______________ (to tell) you. I ______________ (to say) that I ______________ (not, to meet) my friends there, but there ______________ (to be) a lot of other people there."

Peter: "So how long ______________ you ______________ (to stay) there?"

Mary: "Well, we ______________ (to leave) the house at 1 pm and we ______________ (to come back) at 7 pm, so we ______________ (to stay) there for about five hours."

Peter: "Weren't you hungry?"

Mary: "A little bit, but that ______________ (not, to matter). It ________ (to be) so much fun. And we ________ (to have) dinner at home after the trip."

Peter. "So you ______________ (not, to take) any food with you and ..."

Mary: "Listen, Peter: We ______________ (to take) some food with us, but it ________ (not, to be) for us. We ______________ (to bring) the carrots and the bread for the animals!"

Peter: "Oh, now I know, where you ______________ (to go). You and your Dad ______________ (to visit) the animals at the zoo!"

Mary: "Yes, you got it."

Exercise 1

1 The Romans **lived/didn't live** in Egypt (= Ägypten).
2 Our grandparents **took/didn't take** the bus to school.
3 In the 16th century Shakespeare **wrote/didn't write** the play *Romeo and Juliet*.
4 The Germans **watched/didn't watch** colour TV in the 1920s.
5 Robert Pattinson **played/didn't play** Edward in *Twilight*.

Exercise 2

Mary: "Hi Peter, you didn't

1 call me last night."
2 say 'Goodbye' after our History class yesterday."
3 give me back my £5 last Sunday."
4 come to my birthday party."

Peter: "I'm so sorry Mary, but I didn't

a find my invitation."
b get my pocket money."
c find your telephone number."
d see that you were there."

1c, 2d, 3b, 4a

Exercise 3

	Lösungsbeispiele:
1 **Did you get to the concert by bus?**	No, I didn't. I rode my bike there.
2 **Did the band leader sing your favourite song?**	Yes, he did.
3 **Did the musicians wear funny clothes?**	No, they didn't. They wore jeans and T-shirts.
4 **Did you go to the concert with your friends?**	No, I didn't. I went there with my family.
5 **Did you know all the lyrics (= Liedtexte)?**	Yes, I did.

Exercise 4

Peter: "Mary, where were you yesterday afternoon?"
Mary: "Ha, you'll never find out where I was yesterday!"
Peter: "Hmmm, let's see. **Did** you **meet** any friends there?"
Mary: "No, I **didn't.** I **went** there with my Dad."
Peter: "So you **didn't see** any other people there?"
Mary: "That's not what I **told** you. I **said** that I **didn't meet** my friends there, but there **were** a lot of other people there."
Peter: "So how long **did** you **stay** there?"
Mary: "Well, we **left** the house at 1 pm and we **came back** at 7 pm, so we **stayed** there for about five hours."
Peter: "Weren't you hungry?"
Mary: "A little bit, but that **didn't matter.** It was so much fun. And we had dinner at home after the trip."
Peter: "So you **didn't take** any food with you and ..."
Mary: "Listen, Peter: We **took** some food with us, but it wasn't for us. We **brought** the carrots and the bread for the animals!"
Peter: "Oh, now I know where you **went.** You and your Dad **visited** the animals at the zoo!"
Mary: "Yes, you got it."

The simple past

EXERCISE 1 Fill in the missing forms.

infinitive	simple past	German	infinitive	simple past	German
to clean	____	____	***to meet***	____	____
____	____	denken	____	____	sparen
____	***ate***	____	____	***made***	____
to give	____	____	***to know***	____	____
____	***fell***	____	____	***spoke***	____

10 P

EXERCISE 2 Put the past tense forms of the following verbs in the correct columns.

to like | to visit | to stop | to stay | to happen | to rain | to land | to help | to end

[-d]	[-t]	[-id]
____	____	____
____	____	____
____	____	____

10 P

EXERCISE 3 Write down what Austin's friends did yesterday.

Matt

Wilson & Gabe

Catherine

Ethan

Marissa

Matt ____________________

Wilson & Gabe ____________________

Catherine ____________________

Ethan ____________________

Marissa ____________________

10 P

EXERCISE 4 Write questions in the **simple past.**

1 the story / how / to end

____?

2 you / the story / to enjoy

____?

3 more / in the book / not to be / ghost stories / there

____?

4 Megan / why / not to buy / the book

____?

5 how long / the story / to be

____?

6 not to frighten / the ghost / you

____?

12 P

EXERCISE 5 Fill in the blanks missing **verb forms.**

not answer	not be (2x)	happen	take
arrive	explain	not hear	tell
ask	get out	run	try
be	not get up	stop	want

A field trip to London

Last week, Mr Brown __________ his class to London on a field trip. He __________ to show his pupils the Tower of London and the Crown Jewels. Everybody __________ very excited and __________ at school early. But at 8 am Matt and Bryan still __________ there. "What __________? __________ they __________ on time?" Mr Brown __________. "They __________ at the bus stop this morning," Ashley __________ an angry Mr Brown. So, Mr Brown __________ to call Matt and Bryan's parents, but they __________. Suddenly, a car __________ in front of the school and Matt and Bryan __________. They __________ to their classmates and __________: "We __________ the alarm clock because our cat was sitting *(= saß)* on it!"

17 P

Connectives and connective phrases

Exercise 6 Connect the following sentences. Use the connectives **and, but, because** and the connective phrases **first, then, finally.** Rewrite the text and put the verbs in brackets in the correct simple past form.

Ashley (to go) to London. She (not to have) a present for her brother Jason's birthday.	____________________ ____________________
She (to look) everywhere. She (not to find) a good gift.	____________________ ____________________
Ashley (to go) to the book shop. She (to go) to the big department store. She (to go) to the pet shop.	____________________ ____________________ ____________________
There, Ashley (to buy) a new bowl for Mischief, Jason's dog. She also (to get) him a nice card.	____________________ ____________________
At home, she (to put) the present under her bed. It (not to be) Jason's birthday yet.	____________________ ____________________
On his birthday, Jason (to open) his present. He (to be) very happy about the new bowl for Michief.	____________________ ____________________ ____________________

9 P

Exercise 7 Translate into English.

1 Wir sind mit den Rädern an den Strand gefahren und gingen schwimmen.

____.

2 Danach haben wir heiße Schokolade in Mo's Café getrunken, weil uns so kalt war.

____.

3 Jenny beschloss, wieder nach Hause zu fahren, aber ich wollte noch bleiben.

____.

4 Schließlich radelten wir zurück, weil es anfing, dunkel zu werden.

____.

16 P

How much? / how many? / much / many / some / any / no

EXERCISE 8 A look into the fridge. Finish the sentences. Choose one product for each sentence.

milk | eggs | orange juice | butter | carrots | yoghurts

1 There is no ____________________.
2 There isn't much ____________________.
3 There aren't any ____________________.
4 There are some ____________________.
5 There isn't any ____________________.
6 There are some ____________________.

6 P

EXERCISE 9 **Some** or **any / no?**

1 It is so hot today. The flowers probably need ____________ water.
2 Mary wants to make pancakes, but she doesn't have ____________ eggs.
3 Ty can't cut out his art project. There aren't ____________ scissors.
4 I can't send you an e-mail. I have ____________ account.
5 Let's go to the cinema. They are showing ____________ good movies.
6 I don't know what to draw? Have you got ____________ ideas?
7 You look cold. Can I offer you ____________ hot tea?
8 This classroom is empty. There are ____________ pupils.

8 P

EXERCISE 10 Peter the rabbit. Matt is looking after Gabe's rabbit Peter for the weekend.

Complete the dialogue. Use **how much / many** and **some, any** or **no** in the answers.

Matt: "________________ carrots does Peter eat?"
Gabe: "One or two a day. There are ________________ carrots in this bag."
Matt: "________________ grass must I give him?"
Gabe: "He loves grass. But I didn't bring ________________ grass."
Matt: "________________ time can he spend outside?"
Gabe: "It's still cold outside. Please don't let him spend ____________ time outside.
Matt: "________________ other pets have you got?"
Gabe: "I have got ________________ other pets. One rabbit is enough!".

8 P

✓ ↩ ?

Exercise 11 The new student. Listen carefully and tick the correct answers.

	true	false	not in the text
1 School starts at 8 am.			
2 Mrs Engelmeyer teaches Biology.			
3 Mr Bogle is Haley's favourite teacher.			
4 Haley was surprised that somebody was sitting in her seat.			
5 There are only girls in Haley's class.			
6 Abby wants to be in the football team.			
7 She likes singing.			
8 Abby has got a brother at Woodridge Middle School.			
9 Haley was angry at Abby all day.			
10 Haley has got a pet.			
11 It was sunny.			
12 The school bell rings three times before school starts.			

12 P

Exercise 12 Listen again and answer the following questions in complete sentences.

1 Does Haley like Mrs. Schaffer? Why / why not? ______________________

____

2 Where did Abby live before? ______________________

____

3 Which instruments does Abby play? ______________________

____

4 What are the girls going to do after school?______________________

____

8 P

Auswertung Trage rechts deine Gesamtpunktzahl ein und vergleiche.

☺ 126 – 95 points	😐 94 – 64 points	☹ 63 – 0 points

TOTAL SCORE 126

Exercise 1

to clean, cleaned, putzen	**to meet, met,** treffen
to think, thought, denken	**to save, saved,** sparen
to eat, ate, essen	**to make, made,** machen
to give, gave, geben	**to know, knew,** wissen (kennen)
fall, fell, fallen	**speak, spoke,** sprechen

Exercise 2

[-d]: stayed, happened, rained [-t]: liked, **stopped** (2 P), helped
[-id]: visited, landed, ended

Exercise 3

Matt **fed [fed]** the chickens. Wilson and Gabe **bought** football tickets. Catherine **read** a magazine. Ethan **dreamt** about his birthday. Marissa **wrote** an e-mail.

Exercise 4

1 How did the story end?	4 Why didn't Megan buy the book?
2 Did you enjoy the story?	5 How long was the story?
3 Weren't there more ghost stories in the book?	6 Didn't the ghosts frighten you?

Exercise 5

took | wanted | was – arrived | were not (weren't) | happened | Didn't – get up - asked | were not (weren't) – told | tried - didn't answer | stopped - got out | ran - explained – didn't hear

Exercise 6

went – because – didn't have | looked – but – didn't find | First, – went | Then – went | Finally – went | bought – and – got | put – because – wasn't | opened – and – was (0.5 p for each new verb form; 0.5 p for each connective)

Exercise 7

1 We rode our bikes to the beach and went swimming. **2** Then, we drank some hot chocolate in Mo's Café because we were so cold. **3** Jenny decided to go back home, but I wanted to stay. **4** In the end, we rode our bikes back because it started to get dark.

Exercise 8

1 milk / orange juice / butter	4 eggs / carrots / yoghurts
2 milk / orange juice / butter	5 milk / orange juice / butter
3 eggs / carrots / yoghurts	6 eggs / carrots / yoghurts

Exercise 9

1 some **2** any **3** any **4** no **5** some **6** any **7** some **8** no

Exercise 10

How many | some | How much | any | How much | any | How many | no

Exercise 11

1 true **2** not in the text **3** false **4** true **5** false **6** true
7 true **8** false **9** false **10** true **11** not in the text **12** false

Exercise 12

1 No, she doesn't because she is very strict.
2 Abby lived in London.
3 Abby doesn't play any instruments.
4 The girls are going to eat some ice cream and take Haley's dog for a walk.

Grammatical term **(Grammatischer Begriff auf deutsch)**	***Example*** **(Englisches Beispiel)**	**→ Modul(e)**
adjective (Adjektiv)	*a **sunny** day; a **good** song*	
adverb (Adverb)		
adverb of frequency (Adverb der Häufigkeit)	***always, often, sometimes, never***	24, 25, 29, 39
adverbial phrase (Adverbialbestimmung)		
of place (des Orts)	*I eat lunch **at home.***	29, 31
of time (der Zeit)	*We go to the zoo **on Sunday.***	29, 31
article (Artikel)		
definite (bestimmt)	***the: The** house is pink.*	19
indefinite (unbestimmt)	***a, an: A** banana is tasty and **an** apple too.*	19
auxiliary (Hilfsverb)		
can	*You **can** play football with your friends.*	15, 17, 31
must	*I **must** help my Mum in the kitchen.*	15, 16, 31
to do	*What **do** you eat for dinner?*	11, 25, 30, 32
mustn't	*You **mustn't** run in the museum.*	18
needn't	*He **needn't** learn vocabulary. He knows it all.*	18
to be *(sein;* kann Voll- oder Hilfsverb sein)	*I **am,** she **is,** we **are*** *We **are** singing a song.*	3, 4, 10, 13, 22, 23, 26, 29, 31, 37, 38
connective (phrase) (Konjunktion/satzverbindende Wendung)	***First** he gets the ball, **then** he runs towards the goal, **finally** he scores.*	33
demonstrative pronoun (Demonstrativpronomen)	***this/that** book, **these/those** skates*	5
to do *(machen;* kann Voll- oder – ins Deutsche nicht übersetztes – Hilfsverb sein)	*I always **do** my homework.* ***Do** you like holidays?*	11, 25, 30, 32
genitive (Genitiv)		
s**-genitive* (Genitiv mit ***s)	*My friend**'s** house is nearby.*	12
of**-genitive* (Genitiv mit ***of)	*The name **of** my school is "South Gosforth."*	12
have got *(haben, besitzen)*	*I **have got** a cat and she **has got** a dog.*	13, 14, 31, 37
imperative (Imperativ)	***Come** in. **Don't be** late.*	11

Grammatical term **(Grammatischer Begriff auf deutsch)**	***Example*** **(Englisches Beispiel)**	**→ Modul(e)**
infinitive (Infinitiv, Grundform)	***(to) go, (to) sleep, (to) learn, (to) have***	3, 22, 23, 24, 25, 26, 36, 37, 38, 39
long form (Langform)	***I am, she is*** *reading,* ***we do not*** *sleep*	3, 4, 13, 14, 22, 23, 39
much/many (Mengenangaben: *viel/viele*)	***much*** *information,* ***many*** *children*	34
negative (form) (Verneinung)	*We* ***don't like*** *homework.*	4, 6, 11, 14, 18, 23, 25, 35, 37, 39
noun (Nomen)	***boy, class, pencil case, idea***	9, 13, 34
number (Zahl)	***two thousand and twelve, one million***	21
object (Objekt)	*Mary gives* ***Jim*** *a* ***book.*** *We like* ***ice cream.***	29, 31, 32
object pronoun (Objektpronomen) *direct* (direkt) *indirect* (indirekt)	***me, you, him/her, it, us, you, them*** *Can you see* ***me?*** *Can I talk to* ***you?***	 20 20
ordinal number (Ordnungszahl)	*Her birthday is on the* ***seventh*** *of August.*	27
past tense/simple past (einfache Vergangenheit/Präteritum)	*Yesterday I* ***walked*** *to school.*	36, 37, 38, 39
personal pronoun (Personalpronomen)	***I, you, they*** *etc.:* ***You*** *are my best friend.*	1, 20
plural (Plural)	*dog**s**, m**e**n,* ***mice,*** *famil**ies***	1, 3, 4, 5, 6, 9, 12, 22, 23, 34, 35
possessive determiner (Possesiv-begleiter/Possessivpronomen)	***my, your, our*** *etc.:* ***My*** *mum is the best.*	2
preposition (Präposition)	***at*** *home,* ***on*** *Sunday,* ***into*** *the pencil case*	7, 8
present progressive/present tense (Verlaufsform des Präsens)	*He* ***is playing*** *my favourite song.*	13, 22, 23, 26, 31, 32
present tense (Präsens) *simple present* (einfaches Präsens) *present progressive* (Verlaufsform des Präsens)	 *He* ***likes*** *to play the guitar.* *He* ***is playing*** *my favourite song.*	 16, 24, 25, 26, 32, 37, 39 13, 22, 23, 31, 32

→

Grammatical term **(Grammatischer Begriff auf deutsch)**	*Example* **(Englisches Beispiel)**	→ **Modul(e)**
question (Fragesatz)	***Is this your bag?, What are you doing?***	1, 4, 6, 10, 14, 15, 16, 17, 23, 25, 30, 31, 32, 37, 39
question word (Fragewort)	***Who?, What?*** *etc.:* ***What*** *is your name?*	4, 23, 25, 30, 31, 32
short answer (Kurzantwort)	***No, he isn't.***	4, 6, 10, 14, 17, 23, 37, 39
short form (Kurzform)	***I'm, she's*** *reading,* ***we don't*** *sleep*	3, 4, 5, 10, 13, 14, 16, 22, 23, 37, 39
signal word (Signalwort)		
simple present (für einfaches Präsens)	***always, usually, often, sometimes, never***	26
simple past (für einfache Vergangenheit/Präteritum)	***an hour ago, last week, yesterday***	36
simple past/past tense (einfache Vergangenheit/Präteritum)	*Yesterday I* ***walked*** *to school.*	36, 37, 38, 39
simple present/present tense (einfaches Präsens)	*He* ***likes*** *to play the guitar.*	16, 24, 25, 26, 32, 37, 39
singular (Singular)	***a dog, an ice cream, one tree***	1, 3, 4, 5, 6, 9, 12, 22, 23, 24, 25, 26, 34
some/any (Mengenangaben: *einige, etwas*)	*There are* ***some*** *apples, but there aren't* ***any*** *pears.*	35
subject (Subjekt)	***I*** *go to school.* ***We*** *like ice cream.*	4, 29, 31, 32
there is/there are *(es gibt)*	***There is*** *a cat, but* ***there are*** *no dogs.*	6
this/that, these/those (Demonstrativpronomen)	***this/that*** *book,* ***these/those*** *skates*	5
verb (Vollverb, Tätigkeitswort)	*I* ***watch*** *a movie at the cinema.*	3, 4, 22, 23, 24, 25, 26, 29, 31, 37, 38
word order (Wortstellung im Satz)		4, 8, 14, 15, 16, 17, 18, 23, 24, 25, 26, 29, 30, 31, 32, 33, 39

Ihre Meinung ist uns wichtig

Wir entwickeln Lernhilfen und Arbeitsmittel in engem Kontakt mit Schulpraktiker/innen und Nutzer/innen. Deshalb sind uns Ihre **Anregungen** und **Wünsche**, aber auch Ihr **kritisches Urteil** besonders zu neuen Produkten wichtig und willkommen.

Meine Angaben beziehen sich:

☐ auf den vorliegenden Band (978-3-06-150195-2)

☐ auf ein anderes Produkt, nämlich ______________________________

Wie beurteilen Sie folgende Aspekte des Produkts:	++	+	0	–	– –
Übersichtlichkeit/Layout					
Themenauswahl/Inhalte					
Aufbau/Gliederung					
Übungsangebot					
Niveau/Schwierigkeitsgrad					
Altersangemessenheit					

Was ist Ihnen außerdem noch wichtig?

____

____

Die Absenderin / der Absender ist (bitte Zutreffendes ankreuzen):

☐ Lehrer/in
bitte angeben: Fächer ______________________
Klassenstufen ______________________

(Schule/Schulstempel – bitte immer angeben)

☐ Seminarleiter/in

☐ Fachbetreuer/in

☐ Referendar/in

☐ Lehramtsstudent/in

☐ Elternteil

☐ Nachhilfelehrer/in

– Antwort –

Cornelsen Verlag
Service Center
14328 Berlin

Bitte senden Sie uns diese Seite an die links nebenstehende Adresse zurück. Noch einfacher geht es per **Fax** unter **0180 / 1 21 20 12** (3,9 ct/min aus dem Festnetz der Telekom. Mobilfunkhöchstpreis: 42 ct/min)

Name und Privatanschrift

____
Name

____
Straße, Hausnummer

____
PLZ, Ort

____
Telefon

____
E-Mail-Adresse

☐ Ja, informieren Sie mich bitte per E-Mail gezielt über Ihr Verlagsprogramm.